— Thirty Years of Fly-Fishing Insight —

Jim McLennan

fusionbooks

Calgary, Alberta

Published by
Fusion Books
2815 12th Street NE
Calgary, AB T2E 7J2
www.flyfusionbooks.com

Library and Archives Canada Cataloguing in Publication

McLennan, Jim, 1953-
Water marks : thirty years of fly-fishing insight / Jim McLennan.

ISBN 978-0-9784786-0-5

1. Fly fishing. I. Title.

SH456.M35 2008 799.12'4 C2008-900109-5

Editor: Derek Bird
Copy Editor: Jenn Nagel
Design: Terry Paulhus
Illustrator: Al Hassall
Cover Photo: Jim McLennan
Inside Jacket Photo: Dave Jensen
All photos by Jim and Lynda McLennan

Printed in Canada

ACKNOWLEDGEMENTS

A great many fine magazine editors worked with these stories originally, and I thank them for bringing the poorest parts of my writing up a notch and for leaving the best parts alone. These include Derek Bird, Keith Gardner, Dave Hughes, Aaron Kylie, Chris Marshall, Anne Mitchell, Steve Probasco, Ross Purnell, Craig Ritchie and Patrick Walsh.

I'd like to also acknowledge the efforts and initiative of Fusion Books, including Chris, Derek, Jennifer, Gary and Sandra Bird, Jenn Nagel, and Don MacEachen.

Al Hassall's art has illuminated many writers' words over the years. I'm pleased to be one of those writers, and I'm especially pleased that Al's work appears in this book. Special thanks also to John Randolph.

Finally, thanks to my wife Lynda, for 30 years of love, friendship and great photographs of our fly-fishing adventures.

CONTENTS

FOREWORD

I have known Jim McLennan since 1982, when he opened Country Pleasures, the first flyshop in Calgary. Then, in 1985, he wrote a piece for *Fly Fisherman*, and I learned that Jim was that rare bird, a man who fly fishes well and writes about it with professional advice in an open and direct style. In 1996 he published *Trout Streams of Alberta*, followed in 1998 by a revised and updated version of his first book, *Blue Ribbon Bow*. During that period ('82-'98) fly fishing enjoyed its greatest growth in history, thanks to the movie *A River Runs Through It*, which explored family values taught and lived through fly fishing.

Working from his flyshop—guiding, teaching, and writing—Jim McLennan became the Johnny Appleseed of fly fishing in the Alberta region and as far west as British Columbia and as far south as the American Rockies. He also became a valued contributor to *Fly Fisherman* magazine because, like the other mentors of our sport, he was a man of his river, with established roots in modern fly fishing, and he had new and important things to say about what we do and why and how we do it.

As an editor, I search for men and women who speak from the heart of fly fishing, writers who can explain a complex sport in uncomplex ways, and whose values represent and instruct us in what makes fly fishing the new-age sporting religion of the "neoconservationists."

That sentence describes a complex modern conundrum: How can we fly fishers ethically enjoy a formerly consumptive sport without consuming the prey that we pursue and without suffering from advancing cultural guilt? Should we be doing what we are doing? If so, then how should we comport ourselves and what should our public and private values be? We know what our Victorian British mentors taught us about fly fishing, but we are now skating on new (post-modern) ice. So, who are our new prophets and cultural mentors?

Jim McLennan speaks from his river—the Bow, but his message has become universal among fly fishers everywhere: He speaks to, and for, us all. He is a modern respected elder.

I use the word "neoconservationists" because modern fly fishers have become the new special-interest conservationists: They understand stream ecosystems in a highly informed, science-based way. And they are willing and able to man the barricades to protect and restore the waters that are threatened by Industrial Man. These new generations of fly fishers carry in their hearts the new values: They are not just "fishermen"; they are fly-fishing naturalists. They are the political Tenth Legion of an army that fights to protect and restore nature's precious veins and arteries—her rivers and streams and the trout that inhabit them.

If this sounds precious or over-stated, talk to a fly fisher. He will tell you that fly fishing is about re-creation (of yourself), re-connection (with nature), relaxation, camaraderie (with others who share our values), quietude, adventure, problem solving—and preservation, of the places, values and memories that we share. That is what this book is all about.

Some of the chapters were first published in *Fly Fisherman*. In fact the chapter "Handling Drag" appeared in our March 1985 issue. When I re-read it after 22 years, I re-learned lessons that will never become stale—to me and to any new-generation fly fisher. It is a how-to piece on the basics, the fundamentals of successful dry-fly presentation, and it is typical of the book's section on how to fly fish successfully.

Other sections, equally important, are on bugs and fish, great places that McLennan has fished, and fly-fishing personalities.

For this reader, the core section of this book discusses fly-fishing values. It is here that McLennan, without preaching, sets forth his modern credo. The book offers a sampling of the "The Best of McLennan," but it should spur the reader to reading his previous books.

It has been said that fly fishing is the only sport that has its own literature. The McLennan books have earned high ranking in the extensive library of fly-fishing literature.

John Randolph, Editor and Publisher, Fly Fisherman *magazine*

PREFACE

When it dawned on me recently that I have been writing fly-fishing stories for outdoor magazines for nearly 30 years, my first reaction was to check the math. Then, when the depression lifted, I began thinking about gathering some of the stories and publishing them as a collection. This is it.

The pieces here have been selected from the writing I've done in that period and are grouped under five headings. The stories in *Where* deal with places, while those in *How* deal with fly-fishing methods. *Bugs and Fish* is a bit of a catch-all section for pieces that don't clearly belong in any of the others, but most of the stories are about specific fish or insects, or the imitations of the latter that we use to fool the former. The pieces in *Why* address what might be called the philosophy of fly fishing, and since it's my book, I'm afraid you're stuck with my philosophy. The section *Who* contains profiles of fly-fishing people.

These pieces were all written to stand alone, so readers don't need to start at the beginning and proceed through in order. In fact, I hope you'll skip around through the menu. Most of the pieces appear largely in their original form though all were subjected to a certain amount of tinkering, which is the unavoidable addiction of all writers. In some cases two stories on the same topic were combined into one. Because of the large time period from which these pieces were taken, some of the information is no longer true or up-to-date. In most cases this has not been updated unless there was a need to do so to avoid confusion. The stories simply reflect what was said and what was (hopefully) true at the time they were written.

You'll also probably notice contradictions between pieces. I have not tried to hide these, and I rationalize them simply as being proof that opinions change.

With the exception of "Ditching the Script," which is previously unpublished, the stories in this book have appeared in various Canadian and American fly-fishing and outdoor magazines, including *The Alberta Fishing Guide*, *American Angler*, *The Canadian Fly Fisher*, *Fishing World*, *Fly Fisherman*, *Fly Fishing and Tying Journal*, *Fly Fusion*, *Gray's Sporting Journal*, *Northwest Fly Fishing*, *Outdoor Canada*, *Real Outdoors*, and *Sporting Classics*. The original publication date appears at the beginning of each piece.

A unique aspect of this book is the fact that colour photographs appear throughout. Some of these are intended to support or illustrate the stories where they appear, and others are simply intended to portray the beauty that is inherent to the sport of fly fishing. Like the stories, the photographs have been gathered from those Lynda and I have taken over the last 30 years or so.

In these stories you'll find some of the places, experiences, fish, and people that have kept fly fishing on my mind for over forty years. They are marks made by water.

Jim McLennan
October 2007

Section One: Where

"...so a relevant, but apparently tricky question is, where are the little fish? The answer is not clear, at least not to me. Everyone I asked seemed quite sure, but the answers were all different. The little fish then, are either in the extreme upper sections of the streams, in the extreme lower sections of the streams, killed by spring floods, or eaten by eels."

WHERE

CHAPTER 1

Trout Towns

2006

There's a pleasing situation that's developed within fly-fishing culture over the last 25 years or so. In the right circumstance, which is to say in a place where there is fly fishing available that is either extremely abundant or extremely good, the reputation of the fishing transfers by some sort of osmosis to the nearest town, where it is embraced and assimilated into the community's identity.

One of the best examples is Ennis, Montana. Located on the great Madison River, Ennis has a permanent population of just 1000 people, but a good many of them are involved in the business of fly fishing, by way of fly shops, guide services, and fishing lodges. You get your first hint of Ennis's status as a bona fide Trout Town when you notice all the trout and fly logos that adorn ranch gates and mailboxes. You get a stronger hint still when you pull into town off the road from Virginia City. As you slow down for the four-way stop, your eyes are drawn to a grassy enclosure wherein stands a larger-than-life sculpture of a fly fisherman casting a long line toward the Madison.

Another community that qualifies is Turangi, on the North Island of New Zealand. There a billboard unabashedly pronounces the town "Trout Fishing Capital of the World." The tiny hamlet of Craig, Montana makes the list too. On any summer weekend, driftboats in Craig outnumber residents by at least three-to-one.

It takes more than proximity to good fishing for a town to achieve this lofty status. First, it can't be too big, for with size comes diversity and sophisticated tourism marketing that generally overlooks our quaint little sport. This is why places like Denver and Boise don't make it, even though they're near great fishing.

Second, a genuine Trout Town isn't a full-bore, all-purpose tourist town. This lets out places like Jackson Hole, Aspen, and Sun Valley.

Third, the town must consider fly fishing crucial to its identity. Bozeman, Montana has great and diverse fly fishing, at least five fly shops, and dozens of guides and outfitters. It's become a trendy place lately, with a hot real estate market and an abundance of art galleries, fancy restaurants, and cappuccino bars. Bozeman is also a college town, a fact that puts a deep imprint on its personality. Bozeman is a great place from which to base a fishing trip, but it's not a true Trout Town. Just over the hill, though, is Livingston—less trendy, more gritty, and definitely a Trout Town. Its pedigree is anchored by two fly-fishing institutions: the Yellowstone River

and Dan Bailey's Fly Shop. The latter was established when the river drew the man to the town in 1938. Livingston has also been home to celebrated fly-fishing writers and artists like Charles Waterman and Russell Chatham. What clinches it for me, though, is Martin's Café. Martin's is the decidedly un-trendy café in the old train station, and one of only a few places where you can get sourdough pancakes for breakfast. At Martin's, the chicken fried steak special is posted on a chalkboard along with fishing conditions and hatches on the Yellowstone River.

In spite of an abundance of great fly fishing, there aren't many real Trout Towns north of the border. Calgary might well be Canada's fly-fishing capital, but it's far too big and busy to include the great fishing in the Bow River part of its persona. A true Trout Town flaunts its association with fly-fishing. Those closest to making the cut in western Canada may be Kamloops, B.C., and Blairmore, Alberta.

For those readers who wish to conduct their own research into the authenticity of an alleged Trout Town, I provide the following helpful guidelines:

1. If there are more than three pickup trucks with driftboats parked at the bar on the edge of town after 10:00 p.m., you could be in a Trout Town.
2. Randomly stop somebody on Main Street and ask where the fly shop is. If the response is, "Which one?" you're probably in a Trout Town.
3. While you're having breakfast, ask the 18 year-old gum-chewing waitress with a ring in her nose how the fishing is. If she gives you a short discourse on the idiosyncrasies of the Pale Morning Dun hatch, you're definitely in a Trout Town.
4. If you spot a woman in chestwaders pushing a shopping cart down the aisle of a grocery store, and nobody's giving her a second glance, you're probably in Ennis.

CHAPTER 2

Trout Hunting in New Zealand

1993, 1995

I had come halfway around the world for this and now here I was, staring through some wrinkled water at a small, white rock. My guide, Bob Vaile, was staring at it too. It wasn't an especially interesting white rock, and offered little to recommend itself except for the fact that it resided deep in a freestone river on the South Island of New Zealand, and the brown trout there happen to like white rocks.

Vaile's theory is that the fish often lie just downstream of a pale rock or a light patch of weeds to get a better background against which to view the bugs that drift and curl their way through the pools.

After a time the rock seemed to change shape. First it was circular, but then it had a dark wedge missing from the bottom edge – a wedge the size and shape of a trout's nose. I could see nothing else to suggest the presence of a fish, but you can convince yourself of anything if you try hard enough, so I advised Bob of my hunch and he said it was worth a cast to find out. In New Zealand you're sometimes not sure if you've seen a fish or invented one.

I threw a New Zealand version of a Gold Ribbed Hare's Ear Nymph, called a Hare and Copper, about forty feet upstream so the fly would be near the bottom when it drifted over the rock. A few seconds later the wool indicator, six feet up the leader, twisted and shuddered, and I struck. Wonder of wonders, I was attached not to a white rock but to a brown trout – a brown trout large enough to run up to the head of the pool and break the tippet faster than I can describe it.

With your first step into a New Zealand trout stream, you notice a curious blend of the familiar and the exotic. You get the usual burst of adrenaline that kick-starts every day of fishing, but it comes from conflicting stimuli. This is a trout stream, yes; the water feels cool and slick on your waders, there is gravel under your felts, the morning air smells sweet – all standard sensual confirmations of what it is you are about to do. Yet, when you look closely, this isn't at all like a trout stream at home. In fact, the only completely common elements are the moving water and the fish. The vegetation, the landscape, and especially the jungle-like sounds of the birds are all wonderfully new.

Parts of New Zealand might remind you of places in North America – Oregon or Washington, maybe, or perhaps British Columbia or western Alberta – but other parts are totally unique and simply could not be anyplace else. And New Zealand has thousands of trout streams: freestone rivers whose source is mountain snowmelt, streams that flow out of lakes, and spring creeks that seem to bubble out of the hills everywhere. One fishing lodge on the South Island has a regular repertoire of 14 freestone streams and 10 spring creeks – all within a 90-minute drive. I guess if I lived there I'd eventually develop favourites, but it would take a long time to get over the "kid-in-a-candy-shop" problem of wanting to sample everything I could get my waders into.

Though there are places where standard North American streamer and nymph methods can be used (around Lake Taupo on the North Island, for instance), the big deal in New Zealand is sight fishing, which means seeing the fish before casting to it. It's a sensible method because many of the streams have relatively small numbers of fish, and casting to all possible lies would put the fly in barren water most of the time. In addition, because

New Zealand trout have few overhead predators, they don't hold near cover the way our trout do. They are often out in the open rather than tucked under banks or deadfall. So the Kiwis sight-fish both because the clarity of the water and the fish's habits allow it and because the low numbers of fish demand it.

So you walk upstream, on a high bank if possible, looking intently into the water trying to spot a fish. The Kiwi fly-fishing guides are very good at this and they teach you to look for shapes, shadows, and movement much the way a deer hunter does. The shape has to be the right size, pointed at one end and blunt at the other, with the pointed end facing directly into the current. After you've found a qualifying shape, you hope to see it move–preferably side to side, which means the shape is feeding and is, therefore, a fish.

The trout are skittish as bonefish and spook very easily so camouflage and stealth are important. Your clothing should be dull olive or brown camo to blend in with bankside vegetation, and your movements should be deliberate. You look into the water, inspecting every square inch of the stream bottom in front of you before moving ahead a few steps. You must resist the temptation to move quickly. It is intense, hard hunting, and if you're doing it right your eyes will be sorer than your feet at the end of the day. The best visibility comes with sunshine, so you pray for clear skies. Cloud and overcast make an already difficult task even more so.

The good news in all this is that when you find a fish, it will be big. Guides and lodges routinely weigh and record every fish that's caught and released, and the season average in most areas is between four and five pounds and ten-pounders, if not expected, are within the realm of possibility.

Because you don't know how many fish you're going to find (but you know it won't be too many), you can't be casual, cocky, or cavalier when you find one. The guide has worked hard and he'd prefer that you didn't blow it. So once a fish is found, a plot is carefully hatched and all possibilities considered before the first cast is made: Is the fish feeding or just lying on

the bottom doing nothing? How deep is he? Should it be a dry fly or a nymph? Where should I stand? Will the fly drag? Where will the fish go when I hook him? How's my hair look for the photograph afterward? Each fish becomes a project, because any fish might be the fish of a lifetime.

If the trout is in more than three feet of water, it is probably a candidate for a weighted nymph, but if it's in a shallower spot, it might eat a dry like a Royal Wulff or an Adams. And if he likes your Royal Wulff or Adams, he comes to it in slow motion, tilting and drifting back deliberately, confidently, like a smooth outfielder tracking a lazy fly ball. It seems that he will never get there. But finally, when you've counted the spots on his broad, gold shoulders, he intercepts the fly with a quiet, dignified *splut*. It is, as they say, the moment of truth. You must delay striking until the fish has taken the fly and turned back down with it, and that friends, is all but impossible the first few times it happens. You'll probably strike too fast and take the fly away from the fish, and that's when the festivities begin.

You go straight into the song and dance routine that Kiwi guides see from all their clients at least once. It features cursing and foot stomping, with a chorus that goes like this: "I don't believe it! I took it away from him!" The guide will turn away at this point because he doesn't want you to know he's smiling, and because he's already started looking for the next fish. And, if he's a cruel sort, he might say something like, "Don't worry mate, he was only about seven pounds."

Because everything is stacked in the fish's favour, you must fish carefully to these trout. They become suspicious easily and you can't force-feed them. One day my fishing partner put an Adams over a big brown lying in a shallow South Island riffle. The fish saw it coming, drifted back with the fly an inch from his nose before declining the invitation and dropping back to his lie. "He doesn't want that one," the guide said. "You better change the fly." In the name of science, Mark didn't change but instead made another cast with the Adams. The fish repeated the performance but with a different ending. We could almost see the light-bulb of recognition go on in his head,

for when he had finished his second inspection he slowly and calmly left the pool with body language that said, "What do you take me for?"

One of many fascinating things about New Zealand trout fishing is the fact that the size of the stream seems to have no bearing on the size of the fish that live in it. It doesn't matter if it's a big rolling freestone river or the tiniest of pristine spring creeks, it's rare to see a fish under a couple of pounds. And so a relevant, but apparently tricky question is, where are the little fish? The answer is not clear, at least not to me. Everyone I asked seemed quite sure, but the answers were all different. The little fish then, are either in the extreme upper sections of the streams, in the extreme lower sections of the streams, killed by spring floods, or eaten by eels. It's an enigma to savour.

Like fishing anywhere, in New Zealand there are great days, and then there are other days. For balance, I'll tell you about one of the other ones. Mark Gruber and I were guided by Dave Heine on a gravelly stream in a large, wide-open valley. Heine spotted brown trout after brown trout only to be amazed at the lengths to which Mark and I went to circumvent any threat of success. Everything that could go wrong for the fishermen and right for the fish did. We had problems with the breeze, with our leaders, with our eyes, and with our flies. Dave said the fish were behaving funny. He lied. Finally, at 4:45 p.m. I caught a fish – the only fish that day. There was a lot of wound-licking on the way home, but in retrospect I have to say that though it was frustrating fishing, it was great fishing. We saw a lot of trout, and if the anglers aren't up to the challenge, whose fault is that?

To get the best possible introduction to New Zealand fishing a person should spend a few days with a guide before trying to fish without one. Though the fishing is simple in principle – sight a fish and then throw a nymph or a dry over him – like most things, experience and the fine points turn it into an art. New Zealand guides may not talk Latin about insects nor quote Schwiebert or Marinaro, but they know their waters and their fish. Their most important tools are their eyes. Very few North Americans spot fish as well as the Kiwi guides because very few North Americans get as much practice as the Kiwis do. After two weeks of staring at shapes in the water, there were still many times when I would sight along the guide's pointing finger and not see anything at all.

New Zealand fly fishing isn't for everyone. It's as much hunting as fishing and consequently won't appeal to people who like to step into the water and cast continuously for hours at a time. There is also abundant opportunity for frustration. You never feel better than when you put it all together and get the fish, but you never feel worse than when you trash a cast or otherwise foul up on a fish. It is either exhilaration or exasperation.

Neither does it produce impressive entries in the "number of fish caught" column of the fishing diary. A good day is a dozen fish spotted, six hooked, and three landed. The appeal is in the "how," rather than the "how many."

But there is a purity to this fishing that is utterly addictive. While in New Zealand for the first time, I noticed a pleasant disconnection from the North American fly-fishing mainstream. While we daily become more infatuated with tackle and technique, the New Zealanders love affair is still with the rivers and the fish. When you find a fish, the river itself seems to say to you: "Here's a wild trout in a wild place. See if you can touch it."

A few years before my first trip, a friend took a leave of absence from his accounting practice to travel the world as a fly-fishing bum. He made stops at British Columbia steelhead rivers, Montana trout streams, Christmas Island, Tasmania, New Zealand and other fly-fishing shrines. When he was done he came home, packed up his stuff and went back to Christchurch to live. We all thought he was crazy. We were wrong.

WHERE

CHAPTER 3

21st Century Bow

2003

It's been called a lot of things in the 30 years since it was discovered by the international fly-fishing community, including "the best dry-fly stream on earth," and "a magnificent accident." It's also been called "the most misunderstood fishery in North America," and even less-flattering things by puzzled fly fishers who wonder what all the fuss is about. Ask around and you'll still find disparate opinions about Alberta's Bow River today. There are many Albertans who fish exclusively on the Bow, and each year they are joined by thousands of visitors who come to Alberta just to fish this river. Yet, other people refuse to fish the Bow, saying it's over-rated and over-fished. Some former fans have quit fishing it because it "ain't what it used to be." And there are those frustrated souls who've fished it for several years and are still trying to find their first fish.

In order to review the state of this fishery today, it might be best to begin with a list of things the Bow River is not. First, it's not a very good place to learn to fly fish. Its large size makes it intimidating and difficult to read, and it requires familiarity with a number of fishing methods. These qualities frustrate beginners, especially those who have decided to take up fly fishing because of the stories they've read and heard about the great fishing on the Bow. This might be a poor analogy, but learning to fly fish on the Bow is a bit like learning to drive at Daytona. Smaller streams are easier to read and are better places to learn.

Second, the Bow is not an easy place to be consistently successful. I've had heart-to-heart conversations with many experienced anglers who had a lot of trouble with this river when they first began to fish it. I think some of them suspected that the hoopla about the Bow River belonged in the same category as Sasquatch stories. Information and experience from other waters – especially small streams – don't transfer well to the banks of the Bow. Don't misunderstand me; there are plenty of anglers who consistently catch trout in the Bow, but none of them got that ability quickly. The gradient on the learning curve has always been and still is, very gentle. It's a river that puts a premium on the concept of "paying your dues," and stubborn persistence, preferably with the help of experienced Bow River anglers is the only answer.

Third, the Bow is neither a reliable nor predictable fishery. It's very difficult to know what to expect from it. Conditions can change from one day to the next, thanks to the volatility of weather and water conditions, but that's not really the problem. The problem is that even when conditions don't change, the quality of the fishing can. The fishing can turn off (or on) quickly, and nobody has figured out who throws the switch. The fishing also changes from year to year, with no apparent reasons or hints in advance. In order to address the unpredictable nature of the fishing, the angler must be versatile. A guy who is comfortable and competent with a number of streamer, nymph, and dry-fly methods will usually find a way to catch fish, even if it's not the way he expected to catch them.

The water between Calgary and Carseland produces rainbow and brown trout of larger average size than nearly any other trout stream on the continent. This is where the big fish live, and this is where the greatest numbers of anglers are found. I'm fascinated by conversations centered on the topic of crowding on the Bow. I know people who have stopped fishing this part of the river entirely because it's too crowded. I also know people who choose to fish this water specifically because it's not crowded. Huh? Clearly the issue of crowding is subjective and comparative. Crowded for whom? Crowded compared to what?

There are more people fishing the Bow below Calgary today than there have ever been, but the greatest increase recently has come not from visitors but from local anglers. This should not be a surprise. After all, there are twice as many people living in Calgary as there were 25 years ago. In the old days you could presume that any driftboat you saw belonged to a guide or outfitter. The professionals are still out there, but they have been joined by a great number of private anglers in their own boats. And why wouldn't they fish a great river that flows through their backyards?

Yet, even with this increase in pressure there are far fewer anglers on this water than on other high-quality western trout streams. The Bighorn, Missouri, Green, Madison, South Platte, San Juan and other rivers receive more angling pressure than the Bow. The Bow of the 21st century is definitely crowded compared to the Bow of 1975; yet the Bow today is not crowded compared to many other great trout streams. So if Yogi Berra were a fly fisherman he might tell us that everybody comes to the Bow

because it's not crowded.

It's true that you won't often find total solitude on the Bow below Calgary. You're going to see some other anglers. If solitude is your goal, there are other places in Alberta where it is more easily found; indeed, this is one of the things that makes Alberta a great place to fly fish. But if you want to spend time on the most lightly-fished river of this quality on the continent, the Bow below Calgary is the place.

The reputation of the Calgary-to-Carseland stretch was built largely on dry-fly fishing. In the late '70s and early '80s it was often possible to use nothing but dry flies for weeks at a time. The question often asked today is, "Is it still a dry-fly river?" The answer is yes, but only on a part-time basis. The consistent dry-fly fishing in the old days was wonderful, but we anglers made the mistake of assuming that it was normal. Twenty-five years later, we know that what's really normal is inconsistent dry-fly fishing. We still have great dry-fly days and great dry-fly seasons on the river, but we know that the following day or the following season may not be as great.

Why is this? Many theories have been offered, some of them mine: Too much water; not enough water. Too much runoff; not enough runoff. Too much weed growth; not enough weed growth. These, and more, have been suggested as reasons for the erratic nature of the dry-fly fishing. Suffice to say that the river has deflated most of these theories several times through the years, and the mystery remains.

Perhaps because of the inconsistent dry-fly fishing, other methods have become more popular. Nymphs and streamers have always had a place in a Bow River angler's arsenal, but in recent years they have become the main weapons. Today nymphs are most consistently effective, and the San Juan Worm and Prince Nymph probably account for more Bow River fish than all other flies. Nymph fishing used to be thought of as a difficult method, but it has become easier lately, thanks to the more common use of strike indicators, extra weight, and sophisticated two-fly rigs. A skilled Bow River nymph angler is effective from a drifting boat and from his feet, and can rack up some serious numbers.

When I began fishing this part of the river in earnest in the late '70s, few people fished nymphs or dry flies. The Bow then was a streamer river. Today streamers are less reliable than nymphs, but still usually account for the largest fish. Streamers work best when the water is slightly cloudy, as it is in early summer during the recession of runoff, or anytime the river is clearing after being dirtied by a heavy rain. They are also good on overcast days and early and late in the day when the sun is off the water. There are many good Bow River streamers, including the Bow River Bugger, Clouser Minnow, and Gartside Leech, but the name really doesn't matter. Just be sure the fly is size 4 or 6, and carries a few of the essential ingredients: marabou, rabbit strips, flashabou, and lead eyes. Blend in various colours and combinations and marinate in Bow River water. Streamers are most often fished from a driftboat, but they also take big fish when worked thoroughly through a pool by a wading angler using a sinking tip fly line.

The one thing about this part of the Bow that has remained consistent or even improved throughout its recent history is the size of the fish. This stretch of river has always had big trout. Rich water, abundant food, good habitat, relatively stable water levels, and protective regulations are responsible. The majority of fish caught by experienced fishermen are between 16 and 24-inches long. So when somebody asks me what to expect from the Bow next year, my answer is simple: "The fish will be big." It's the only prediction I'm comfortable making.

More attention is also being directed at the Bow downstream of the Carseland Weir. This section of river, which is largely inaccessible after it enters the Blackfoot Indian Reserve a few miles below the Highway 24 bridge, has traditionally been fished by a relatively small number of anglers. The access difficulties make it available only to anglers with motorboats – generally jetboats, which allow a return upstream after a day drifting and fishing the river.

There are some subtle differences in the river and the fishery downstream of Carseland. It flows through prairie wilderness—wild country with little evidence of human presence. There is a noticeable lack of roads, power-lines, and people. The river is somewhat smaller (because of irrigation withdrawals at Carseland), slower, and gentler. There is less broken water, and consequently less water suited to nymph fishing. The staple method below the weir is fishing streamers from a drifting boat. This method is more consistently effective below Carseland than above, possibly due to lighter fishing pressure on the lower river.

There is also good dry-fly fishing below Carseland, but it seems to begin later in the summer than it does closer to Calgary. There is good hopper fishing along the high banks, and good fishing to rising trout in the long flats. Interestingly, some insects which are important trout food here are not important above the weir. One of these is an as-yet-unidentified pale #14 mayfly that hatches in late summer. Caddis and Blue-winged Olives also bring the fish up.

The restricted access to this part of the river continues to limit the number of anglers, but there are more people fishing this part of the Bow than there were 10 years ago. This is in spite of the fact that there is still discussion over the legality of fishing the river within the Indian Reserve. Some parties view the riverbed as public land, while others feel it is within the jurisdiction of the Indian Band. It seems to depend on when and whom you ask. Some years the band office in Gleichen sells trespass permits that allow fishing through the Reserve, and other years it does not.

So how is the river today, compared to the "good old days" of 25 or 30 years ago? Though we should never become complacent about the condition of our natural resources, I think the Bow River's recent history is largely a feel-good story. The river has more concerned eyes watching it now than ever before, many of which belong to fishermen, and the city and province have begun to realize the Bow's esthetic and economic value. The latest population studies show that the numbers of fish haven't changed significantly. Angling regulations designed to protect large trout and ensure that the Bow below Calgary remains a big-trout river have been in place for 20 years and appear to have been effective. The regulations for the river between Bearspaw and Bassano dams were tweaked in 2001 to simplify them and to maintain or improve protection for spawning-aged trout, while still allowing abundant angling opportunity. While there are those who would like the river to be regulated as completely catch-and-release, the best scientific information seems to tell us that it's not necessary, and that the regulations currently in place will maintain the fishery and the average size of the fish.

Many calamities could have befallen this fishery in the course of Alberta's and Calgary's late 20th century rush to urban sprawl. Someone gazing into a crystal ball in 1975 would not have been considered an alarmist if he'd made dire predictions about the future of the Bow and what it was going to be like in the new century. Thankfully, it appears he would have been wrong.

CHAPTER 4

The North

1998

I recently returned from the first of what I hope will be many trips to fly fish in Canada's North. While the fishing was great, what I brought home that was more important than memories of big fish was a sense of awe. The North is a pretty big place. Roads stop long before geography does. The fact that there's so much of it is one reason why the North still has such great fishing. It's true that Man has made his marks on the North, but they're mostly small nicks compared to the scars we have inflicted on the rest of the planet.

I fished out of a lodge called Camp Grayling, near the Saskatchewan/Northwest Territories border. Lake trout, walleye, pike and Arctic grayling are the featured attractions there, and I was after the latter two.

Both fish were quite co-operative and I felt pretty good about things even though my guide caught approximately five pike with his spinning rod for every one I caught with a fly rod. I still caught quite a few, so that means he caught – well, you get the picture.

Among northern lodge operators there is a growing trend toward recognition of the fragility of their fisheries. It takes decades to grow a four-foot long pike, and only a few minutes to kill one. More and more lodges are enforcing catch-and-release policies on their big fish to ensure that they always have big fish for guests to catch. Back in civilization it would be called protecting your assets.

Camp Grayling has had such a policy for 10 years and it shows in the size of the fish they catch, but guests are still offered the choice of a midday shore lunch of small fish cooked over a campfire. When we left the boat dock the first morning, I noticed that we weren't carrying any "backup" entrees with us. This seemed a little presumptuous to me but when I asked the guide if they ever went hungry at lunch time, he said "only when we forget to bring a rod." Your frame of reference gets a little skewed in the North.

Another example of this is the grayling. No one denies that Arctic grayling are one of the most beautiful of freshwater fish, but in more trendy settings where fly fishing is fashionable and hip, grayling might be considered gullible or even dumb, for they love to come to the surface to take a dry fly – hatch or no hatch. When they're in the mood, you can catch a bunch of them without much trouble. But when you're there, watching them come eagerly up through the pool to nail your dry fly, you begin to appreciate the grayling for what he is – a true wilderness creature, like the wolf or caribou, doing his best to make a go of it in a harsh part of the world.

I've never been obsessed by the North and I'm still not as far as I can tell, but having been there I understand how it can happen. I do know that few people visit the North just once. Read Robert Service and you'll see what I mean.

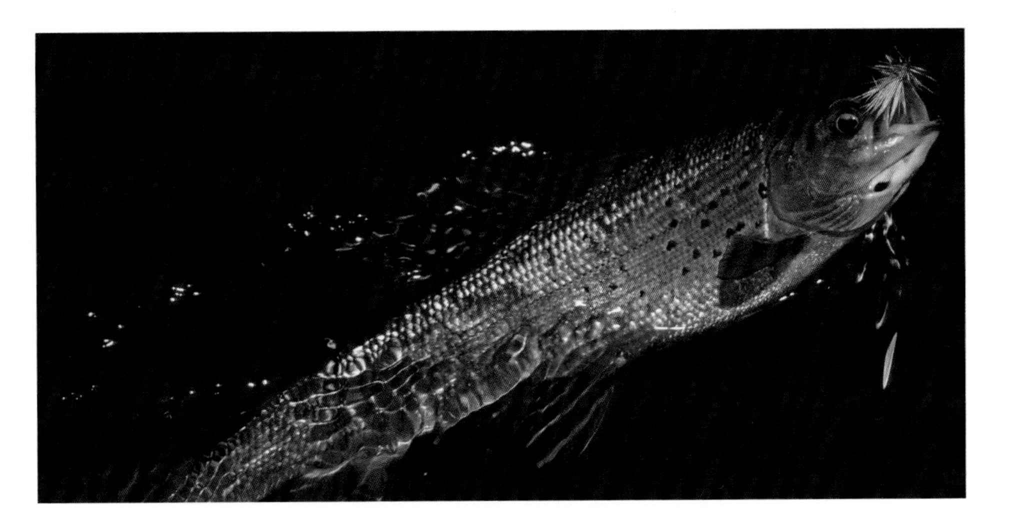

CHAPTER 5

That Oldman River

2001, 2007

Unless you live there, you've had to read the fine print to know much about Alberta's Oldman River. In the world of trout streams, it's like Miss Universe's gorgeous little sister– no press agent, no publicity, and not much fame in spite of its own eminent qualifications. The Oldman, in fact, is overshadowed by not one, but two of its kin: river Bow, which receives most of the adoration that leaks across the 49th parallel from Montana, and river Crowsnest, an Oldman tributary that receives the majority of the remaining attention. But had Mother Nature not put these others in the show, the Oldman River would be the star.

This is supposed to be a fishing story, and I'll try to remember that, but the Oldman is a stream that tugs an author in many directions. The valley of this river has been revered by the Peigan and Blackfoot Indians, settled by the Mounted Police, coveted by the oil and gas industry, defended by environmental groups and flooded by the provincial government. The Oldman's history is still a work in progress, and meditation on such issues as these puts the significance of things like Pale Morning Duns and Green Drakes in new perspective.

But make no mistake, the Oldman River is a trout stream - nearly 100 miles of fine trout stream, in fact. Its first exposure to the fly-fishing world came with a small mention in *McClane's Standard Fishing Encyclopedia* in 1965. In the entry for Alberta, the late A.J. McClane said, "the best stream fishing for rainbow trout in Alberta is to be found in the Bow River for approximately twenty-five miles downstream from the city of Calgary and in the Oldman River as it winds through the foothills northwest of the town of Pincher Creek." Since then, the Bow has received its share of public attention, but the Oldman has remained largely unheralded beyond the borders of Alberta.

The Big Picture

The Oldman begins as numerous named and unnamed trickles of snowmelt along the Continental Divide southwest of the city of Calgary. These join and take on a formal name west of Highway 40, a gravel road running north and south through the edge of the Rockies. Highway 40 is also called the Forestry Trunk Road, and is the major means of access to the high country of the upper Oldman watershed. The Oldman is joined by the Livingstone River, its major northern tributary, and Racehorse Creek before squirting eastward through a narrow opening in the mountains appropriately called the Gap. According to Peigan legend, the Old Man is Na'pi, the Great Spirit and provider of life. It is said that he watches over all he has created from a vantage point near the headwaters of the river. While powerful and omniscient, the Peigans also knew Na'pi to be something of a sly practical joker.

Once through the Gap, the river moves southeastward into the cattle country of Waldron Flats. Part of this lovely area of rolling foothills, rocky outcroppings, grass, and limber pines is called the Whaleback and has been the object of a struggle between environmentalists and advocates of oil and gas exploration. For now the Whaleback is free of such development and its hidden coulees and windy ridges are best known to cowboys, hikers, and fly fishers.

Downstream of Highway 22, the river dekes around the south end of the Porcupine Hills and enters the Oldman Reservoir north of the small farming community of Cowley. In the early 1990s a dam on the mainstem Oldman below its confluence with the Crowsnest and Castle rivers created this huge

irrigation reservoir in the valleys of the rivers. Twenty eight miles of three trout streams were lost. The project was a source of major controversy involving natives, environmentalists, farmers, anglers, angry taxpayers and the provincial government, who ultimately claimed victory. While the dam was under construction, Alberta's legendary cowboy historian, outdoorsman and best-selling author, Andy Russell, told the story of the river and the ill-advised dam in a book called *The Life of a River*. But even Andy Russell, a man appointed to the Order of Canada by Queen Elizabeth, and enormously respected as the most practical of environmentalists, could not slow the engineering juggernaut, and the dam was completed in 1991.

Below the reservoir, the new tailwater portion of the Oldman flows six miles before entering the Peigan Indian Reserve. Below the reserve, the river cuts through the town of Fort Macleod, named for the Northwest Mounted Police colonel who led troops west to quell the activities of American whiskey traders in 1874. Downstream further, the Oldman is joined from the south by the Waterton River, which comes out of Waterton Lakes National Park, and the St. Mary River, which flows north out of Montana. The Oldman bisects the city of Lethbridge before entering the great expanse of prairie. From there it continues northeastward, joining the Bow River and taking on a new name—South Saskatchewan River—west of the city of Medicine Hat.

To a trout fisherman there are three distinct sections of the Oldman. Consider the reach from the headwaters to the Gap as the upper river, the stretch from the Gap to the reservoir as the middle Oldman, and the river from the reservoir to Lethbridge as the lower river.

The Upper Oldman (Headwaters to The Gap)

The upper river smells. In summer the aroma is cool and green, a delicious mix of thin air and evergreens. Friday evenings this is joined by a blend of woodsmoke and gravel dust as campers from Calgary and Lethbridge arrive for the weekend. The upper river flows through high-country wilderness, but it is wilderness made touchable by a well-travelled gravel road. Access is good. Camping is good. Fishing is good.

This part of the Oldman qualifies as a river I suppose, but just barely. Twenty to fifty feet across, it spends most of its time in a narrow gorge. Deep pools, tight corners, and big boulders provide hidey-holes for the fish.

The fish in the upper Oldman are the wilderness trio of westslope cutthroats, bull trout, and mountain whitefish. Cutthroats are the correct and proper fish for wild country like this, and few things epitomize our sport more succinctly than the sight of a gaudy cutthroat pivoting purposefully up through six feet of clear water to take a floating fly. Upper Oldman cutthroats are not large, but fish to about 17 inches can be expected.

The whitefish like Hare's Ears and Golden Stone nymphs dead-drifted deeply through the heads of pools, and the bulls are partial to big gobs of marabou and over-sized Clouser Minnows. But don't get me started on bull trout. Since Alberta-wide no-kill regulations were placed on these fish in 1995, their continued recovery has me headed for full status as a B.T. Junkie.

As bull trout go, those in the upper Oldman are not particularly large either. But remember, large means a bull over 10 pounds. Most of the deep pools in the upper river are patrolled by a couple of pale predators 18 to 24-inches long. The baby cutthroats are nervous.

In a story like this, the author is expected to display his expertise in entomology by knowingly discussing the important insect hatches and the latest high-tech imitations thereof. But we're talking about cutthroats and bull trout here. Cowboy trout. No speak the Latin. The cutts usually eat dries, and the bulls want streamers. For those who consider this a cop-out, experts tell me the most important hatches on the upper Oldman are Golden Stones that show up in mid to late June and Western Green Drake mayflies which arrive a couple of weeks later. Reliable attractor dries, like

Stimulators, Trudes, and Wulffs, are good choices through summer and early autumn.

Following a weekend of heavy fishing pressure, the cutts can get a bit pouty, and they show it by inspecting and then rejecting dry flies. When this happens, they can often be convinced to take a small nymph like a Beadhead Pheasant Tail, drifted a couple of feet below a dainty yarn strike indicator, or fished as a dropper beneath a bushy dry fly.

Though this part of the river opens to angling June 16, the water is usually too cold for good fishing until July. It then fishes well through to early October.

The Middle Oldman (The Gap to Oldman Reservoir)

As the river leaves the Rockies and enters the foothills, it flows through sparsely-populated rangeland where cattle now graze hills that were once home to mammoths and bison. The river gains some nutrients from the land as it flows, and this natural enrichment allows it to grow larger fish. Rainbow trout begin to appear downstream of the Gap and become the dominant fish by the time the river passes the campground on Highway 22. Details are vague, but the rainbows appear to have been introduced to the river in the 1920s and 1930s.

Maybe it's because rainbow trout have a higher IQ than cutthroats, but it seems more important on the middle Oldman to carry a nymph seine, insect I.D. handbook, and fancy flies in your vest. There are still Green Drakes and Golden Stoneflies here, but there are also more of the bugs we've come to associate with richer fisheries—Pale Morning Duns, Blue-winged Olives and caddisflies. The grazing land of the middle Oldman is also prime grasshopper country and the afternoon wind that skims over the jagged lip of the Livingstone range and touches down near the Whaleback brings both blessing and curse to the fly fisher.

On the middle river, the quarters are less cramped than in the confined stretches above the Gap, and a longer rod and slightly heavier line are called for. A nine-foot, 5-wt is perfect. When the fish are looking up, this is lovely dry-fly water, but it's a difficult place to fish nymphs when they're not. There are many sudden changes in depth and some of the deep water is too deep. When I try to nymph this water I spend so much time adding and removing weight, adjusting and re-adjusting the indicator, lengthening and shortening the tippet, that I soon wonder where the fun went. When the trout in the middle Oldman won't look up, I prefer to put on a fast sinking-tip line and a streamer and search the pools for bull trout. That's one way to find bull trout. The other way is more reactive than proactive. You hook a small fish on a dry fly and while you're bringing him in a big bull swoops out from under a rock and tries to take him away from you. This will startle you, but after you calm down you should take the cue and cut back your leader, put on the biggest streamer you own, and make it behave like a cutthroat in trouble. And no, it's not okay to troll the little guy around the pool for awhile before you land him. Even when the bulls don't want to play, you sometimes catch bigger rainbows doing this.

The middle Oldman is not a big river, but it feels like one and sounds like one. Between the Gap and the reservoir the gradient remains reasonably steep. There is some canyon water, some fast water, some big boulders, and some deep pools. There is also some treacherous wading. The rocks are not especially slippery, but there are numerous ledges and sudden drop-offs, all disguised by exceptionally clear water that is at least 50% deeper than it looks.

The Lower Oldman (Oldman Reservoir to Lethbridge)

Some of the best Pale Morning Dun fishing in Alberta occurs in July on the six-mile portion of the Oldman River downstream of the Oldman Dam. I know this is true because so many people have told me about it. I've tried to get in on it myself, but on the July days when I've been there the river has been strangely quiet. And perhaps it's this lack of consistency that best summarizes the fishing on one of the most puzzling pieces of water in Alberta.

While the dam was under construction, government officials were eager to put a positive spin on the loss of large parts of three trout streams, and told anglers that a great tailwater fishery would develop below the dam. And it has. Sort of. When conditions are right, 12 to 20-inch rainbows seem to come out of the woodwork. The problem is that nobody seems able to predict when conditions will be right. Vic Bergman, proprietor of the Crowsnest Angler fly shop in the nearby town of Bellevue, has watched the development of this fishery. "It's a strange piece of water," he says. "You never know from day to day what you'll find. One day the river is clear, the next it's silty. One day fish are everywhere, the next day you can't find them."

In the first few years after the completion of the dam, the river downstream was always clear. But as silt accumulated and settled in the reservoir, the clarity of the water has become more easily affected by wave action. During windy times (of which there are plenty - the reservoir is a favourite with wind-surfers), the river is less than clear.

The river here looks like a miniature version of the Bow downstream of Calgary. Each bend is bounded on one side by a high sandstone cliff and on the other by a low, grassy flat. Hawks wheel above and swallows nest in the cliffs and river banks. This water is big enough for a driftboat or an inflatable raft, and there is a short, pleasant float from the dam to the Summerview bridge just north of the town of Pincher Creek. I especially enjoy this float in August when the hoppers are chattering from the dry, south-facing banks.

Another good time to fish below the dam is in late winter or early spring when ice on the reservoir prevents the wind from stirring the silt. Small nymphs like the South Platte Brassie and Pheasant Tail in size 16 and 18 are good then, as are streamers like the Bow River Bugger fished on a sinking-tip fly line. On warm days there is the prospect of winter dry-fly fishing to heavy midge hatches.

The tailwater section of the Oldman is open to angling year-round and is the only part of the river that is always free of ice.

Six miles below the dam the river enters the Peigan Indian Reserve, where access and fishing are not permitted. Consequently, the rumours are entirely predictable—that is, that the fishing is spectacular. For now, these fish, however many and however big, are off limits to all but Peigan band members and their guests.

Below the reserve the river is something of an unknown quantity. There are still rainbows, whitefish, and bull trout in this part of the Oldman, but the mystery fish is the brown trout. In the 1990s at least two plantings of 100,000 browns were made in the river near Fort Macleod in an attempt to develop a self-sustaining fishery there. The problem is that the fish seem to disappear. A few are caught every year, and fall redd counts indicate some spawning activity, but the general whereabouts of these fish is unknown. Below the city of Lethbridge, the river begins its gradual transition from trout stream to warm-water river, where pike, walleye, and even sturgeon take over from the trout.

* * *

It was late October, and I was on a photographic mission to the Oldman River. My companion and I first visited the headwaters where we captured a few small cutthroats, some photos, and a flat tire. Then we climbed a hill for a spectacular view of the river coming through the Gap, and we finished the day near the Forestry Trunk Road. With just an hour or two left in both the day and in our season, we split up. I walked upstream and fished three pools. In the first, there was a 16-inch cutthroat rising nicely and I caught him. In the second, there was another fish rising that I messed up on. In the third, I hooked another fish on a dry fly. It was a 15-inch cutthroat that seemed to be fighting with unusual vigor. As I dragged him toward me, I saw the reason. A two-foot long bull trout was hot on his tail, charging and snapping and nearly beaching himself on the rock I was standing on as he tried to remove the cutthroat from my possession. I landed and released the cutt, and took the hint. I put on the biggest, ugliest, marabou-iest streamer I could find. Then I pitched it above the spot where the bull had come from and jigged it down the run. The bull slid up behind the pulsing streamer with fins flared and blood in his eye. I watched him open his mouth an inch from the fly before changing his mind, slowly backing away and gliding into the deep. He would not come again to any of the half dozen different streamers I tried. I could see him clearly, lying pale green in the heart of the run, and the image has stayed with me ever since. I know where he is, and I know I'll be back with new flies and new ideas when a new season begins on Na'pi's river.

CHAPTER 6

Fortress Lake

2006

Eastern brook trout are the most beautiful of the trout, and the ones with which North American fly fishing and its grand traditions began. But they're also something of a paradox these days. In their native Northeast, they are regarded with great reverence, but in the West, where their introductions have frequently displaced native trout, brookies are sometimes viewed less favourably, and have recently become targets for the "natives or nothing" movement.

So it's okay to love brook trout if you're "interacting" with them somewhere in the northeastern quarter of North America, which is to say anywhere within their native range. But when you find them out West, you've got to be a little more careful about singing their praises.

This is not too hard to go along with, unless you happen to be "interacting" with two to six-pound brook trout in British Columbia's Fortress Lake. Located deep in the Rockies, Fortress is a long way from the brook trout's native home, yet it's impossible not to love these fish in this place. At Fortress, the boundaries of politically correct biology get a little fuzzy.

Fortress Lake sits just west of the Alberta – B.C. border amongst the most spectacular collection of peaks in the Canadian Rockies: 9,900 foot Fortress Mountain to the north, Serenity Peak and Glacier dominating the west, and leaning out over the lake from 10,000 feet straight up, the scarred face of Chisel Peak.

The first white man to see Fortress Lake was an explorer named Arthur Coleman, who visited the area in 1892. When he viewed the beautiful lake he may not have known nor cared that no fish swam in the emerald water. But others who followed did care. National Parks biologists from Alberta introduced Lake Nipigon "coaster" brook trout to Fortress Lake in the 1930s. In those days, long before the native versus non-native debate had begun, brook trout were often planted in barren mountain lakes in the Rockies of both B.C. and Alberta. Additional stockings were made at Fortress in mid-century, and since then the fish have taken care of business on their own.

My first visit to Fortress was in 1990 when I spent three days photographing the lake for *Gray's Sporting Journal*, and fishing with Mike Furfaro, who owned the lodge there at the time. The fishing was, as they say, "slow, but rewarding." We caught relatively few fish, but their outstanding size easily made up for it. Most of the trout were between two and four pounds, and Furfaro caught one that pushed six. Now if you're a brook trout junkie, you know that the world record was caught in Ontario's Nipigon River ninety years ago. It weighed 14 ½ pounds, which isn't that big if you think in steelhead or bull trout terms, but brook trout just don't get as big as other trout. In most places brookies are tiny jeweled creatures that dance through the clearest water of remote creeks and beaver ponds. Fortress Lake changes the paradigm.

I've had Fortress Lake and its huge brookies on my mind ever since the 1990 trip. I got my second fix in August of 2005, when Dave Jensen, who had just acquired the lodge, invited me to join him for a couple of days of fishing along with his client Brian Whitestone.

We met at the helicopter pad at Abraham Lake just east of Jasper Park on a clear summer morning. Before climbing into the chopper, my mind was on the fishing that waited. I'm a bit single-minded about such things and was mentally going through my checklist to make sure I had everything I needed. But moments later I was not thinking about fly rods or camera gear. The 35-minute flight was the kind of exhilarating experience that Disney and IMAX try to duplicate. We flew up the Cline River, through a magnificent sea of peaks and hanging glaciers, across the Jasper/Banff Highway, past Mt. Athabasca and Mount Columbia, and over the Columbia Icefields. Looking down on the latter, we saw the origins of rivers that drain into three oceans. Scientists call this a hydrological apex and it is the genesis of the Columbia, Athabasca, and North Saskatchewan Rivers.

Before homing in on the long, turquoise oval of Fortress Lake, the chopper went over the Chaba River, which does a perpendicular flow-by of the eastern end of the lake. In an odd twist of geography, the river and the lake, though separated by just a few hundred meters, are not connected. The Chaba River is in Alberta and Fortress Lake is in British Columbia, which means that the continental divide lies on that thin strip of spruce forest between them.

After the chopper dropped us off, we deposited our duffles in the cabins and wolfed down a quick lunch. We took two of the lodge's aluminum boats and motored a short distance down the lake to where Chisel Creek enters. I got there first and anchored off the mouth of the creek. I was ready with a 6-wt fly rod and a 15-foot sinking-tip line. The fly was a size 4 brown Wooly Bugger, and I tossed it into the chop where creek water mixed with lake water. The fly sank for about 10 seconds before I began a slow stripping retrieve. When the fly was halfway back to the boat, a fish took, and I was formally reacquainted with the residents of Fortress Lake. When Dave and Brian arrived a few minutes later, I thought they would anchor beside me, but they had a better idea, which was to beach the boats and fish the creek mouth on foot.

Our original plan was to check the mouth of Chisel Creek and then move down to where the Wood River exits the western end of the lake. But we didn't get in the boats again until it was time to go back to the lodge. I don't know how many two- to six-pound brook trout we caught and released that afternoon and I wouldn't say if I did. On my first trip to Fortress the

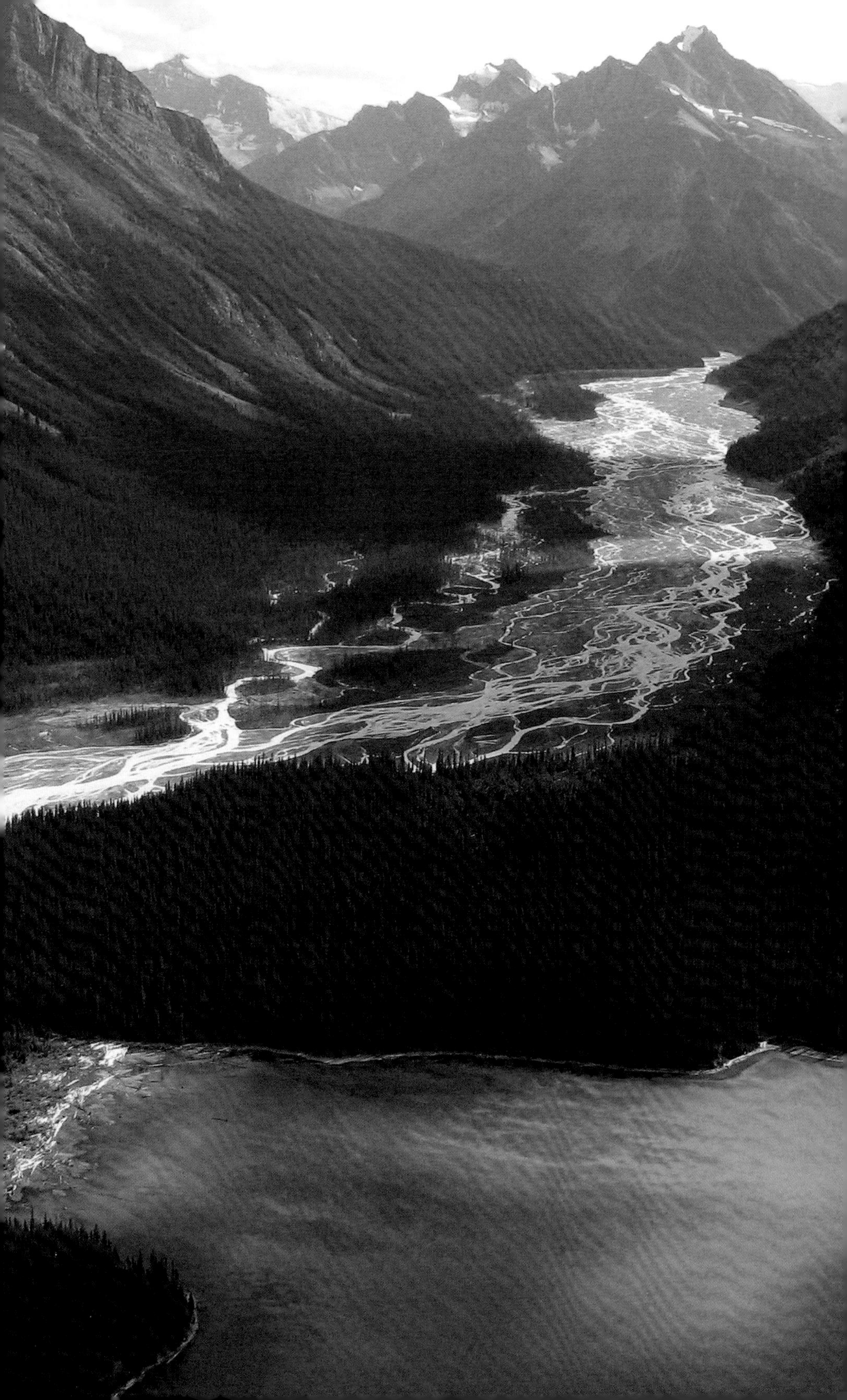

fish were few but large. This day they were plentiful and large. My first photographs were of Brian with a four-pounder. Then I shot Dave with a five-pounder. Then Dave got me with a three-pounder. I finished up by shooting Dave and Brian with matching, bookend four-pounders. The fish were short-bodied, deep, and heavy. Most were 18 to 22-inches long. Their colours ran from a glowing emerald to a smouldery olive, and all had the brook-trout's identification badges: wiggly vermiculations on the backs, pale spots and blue halos on the sides, and brilliant white edges on the pectoral fins. The males' mouths were black inside, kyped and imposing. They fought like all brook trout everywhere – stubborn, persistent, and deep.

I knew from my previous visit that there is very little conventional dry-fly fishing at Fortress. Nobody knows why for sure, but it probably has something to do with a lack of large aquatic insects and an abundance of deep water. But when I realized the fish were stacked at the creek mouth in an aggressive mood, I decided to conduct an experiment. I switched to a full floating fly line with a 9-foot 2X leader, and scammed a beautiful deer-hair mouse fly from Brian. The fish were lying just off the shore, and part of the time I could see them - dark shapes appearing, disappearing, sliding in and out. I cast along the shore to where I had seen the shapes moving, and began to twitch the fly along the surface. I tried to make it behave like Minnie Mouse in trouble, and delivered the play-by-play in my best falsetto: "Mickey, Mickey, help me! They're after me! Help me Mickey!" *Glump*. There was a hole in the water where Minnie used to be, her voice silenced by a three-pound Fortress Lake brook trout. Now that's my kind of dry-fly fishing.

The lake's shoreline is dominated by heavy timber and deadfall, and the bottom drops off quickly from the edges, so fishing from shore is practical in just a few spots, like the mouth of Chisel Creek and the outflow of the Wood River. Otherwise the best fly fishing is done from boats, by anchoring and casting to the mouths of numerous tiny creeks that tumble off the mountainside into the lake. Big wet flies, like Woolly Buggers, leeches, and

Clouser Minnows in size 4 and 6 are reliably effective. These work best when allowed to sink for a count of 10 to 30 seconds before being retrieved at medium-speed.

Fortress Lake can only be accessed by the commercial flights to the lodge or by a 22-kilometer hike that begins at Sunwapta Falls on the Jasper-Banff Highway. Fortress is in B.C.'s Hamber Provincial Park, which has been designated by UNESCO as part of the Canadian Rocky Mountains World Heritage Site. Hikers must stay at one of three small, primitive campsites along the eastern end of the lake. A dedicated angler could pack a float tube in, but its use would be limited to the water near the campsite. Hikers can also arrange to be picked up by boat and taken to stay at the lodge. There are no private flights, no horseback trips, and no motorized vehicle travel to the lake.

After our first day we relaxed over an outdoor dinner and reflected on the rare privilege of being in a place where our biggest concern was deciding where to fish the next day. When it cooled down outside, we moved into the dining room and drank a glass of wine before turning in. In a corner of the dining room is a small fly-tying desk where Brian tied a few streamers for the next day, and on the walls are some photographs and a couple of mounts of big brook trout caught in previous seasons. Giant mounted fish are pretty common in fishing lodges, where guests view them skeptically, thinking "I sure didn't catch any that big." But here you look up at the wall and realize you caught several like that just a few hours ago.

We had originally planned to spend two nights at the lake and be picked up late in the afternoon of our second day. I don't remember whose idea it was, but before long we had decided to make the most of this remarkable experience by staying another day. We used our only means of communication with the outside world – the satellite phone – to advise the chopper to delay our pickup by 24 hours.

It would have been easy to simply go back to the honey hole at Chisel Creek the next morning, but somehow we thought it nobler to go to a different spot. So we summoned our strength and courage and motored past the mouth of Chisel Creek without even looking back. We continued west past a tiny island and on to the outflow of the Wood River. I scanned the steep slopes of spruce and balsam as we rode, hoping to see a grizzly, and in a marshy corner of the lake we watched a cow moose and calf wade and feed.

We pulled in at the end of the lake and walked over to look at the river. All three of us spotted them at the same moment – a group of four or five big brookies lying in a bottom depression where the current gathered momentum as it left the lake. Brian was due up and got into position well above the fish. Dave and I watched and heckled – er – coached, as he cast down and across. He let the current swing his streamer in front of the group, and the outside fish glided over calmly and inhaled the fly. Dave and I burned some memory cards while Brian whooped and fought the fish. We spent a few hours there, taking turns fishing and photographing, and being regularly distracted from our task by the brilliant and changing beauty of Serenity Glacier, which frames the Wood and the west end of the lake.

The following day Dave and I got up early and took photographs on a dead-calm morning when the light was stunning. After breakfast Brian walked back to the mouth of Chisel Creek to fish, while Dave and I made an exploratory run to the eastern end of the lake. Our success was minimal there and we met Brian back at Chisel for the afternoon, where we all caught several more big fish.

I noticed though, that we all fished with a little less intensity this final afternoon, as anglers sometimes do when they find themselves in the unfamiliar position of having little left to prove. We had caught a lifetime's worth of huge brook trout in a glorious setting, and as the afternoon wound down, I tried to gather and hold as much of the experience as I could. I wanted to collect some Fortress Lake magic to take home with me. I know there will be times when I'll need it.

CHAPTER 7

The Other Bow

1999

You're alone, knee-deep in the most beautiful piece of flowing water you've ever seen. A waterfall tumbles from a craggy chunk of the Rocky Mountains into an aqua-blue river behind you, the spray producing a rainbow that ends where your fly line enters the water. Your fly rod is doubled, strained by a five-pound trout that you haul toward your net. A bull elk wades the far side, snorting steam. So, where are you? I hate to be a cynic, but in truth you're either in bed dreaming, or you're in a TV commercial for a beer company, looking too fit, too handsome, and too unfamiliar with that which you're supposed to appear to know how to do. The director bought the fish from the market the day before the shoot.

Advertising folks think this quaint little sport of ours makes a great platform from which to sell stuff, but they've never been troubled much by the pesky notion of authenticity. They have not learned, and undoubtedly wouldn't care if they had, that the best parts of trout streams, the parts where five-pound trout might actually exist, are rarely found in this kind of setting. For unless they're connected to a lake or ocean, western headwater streams are usually too clean, cold and sterile to provide the things trout need, particularly trout like the one in the previous paragraph. There is little connection between Madison Avenue and the Madison River.

There are, however, a few places where the esthetics of the fly-fishing experience begin to approach the perfection of this type of fantasy. One that comes to mind is the South Island of New Zealand, where huge brown trout cruise the pools of crystalline trout streams beneath the Southern Alps. Another is Wyoming's Snake River, where the Grand Tetons provide an inspirational backdrop for great fishing.

Yet another is the upper portion of the Bow River in western Alberta, where anglers fly fish a stunningly beautiful river in the postcard setting of the Canadian Rockies.

The Bow River has received plenty of attention from the fly-fishing press over the last 20 years, but the water you've read about is almost certainly that part downstream of the city of Calgary, where Mother Nature's fallen children have diddled with the river and unwittingly turned a good fishery into a great one. The river below Calgary produces consistently big rainbows and browns and is a required stop on the itinerary of many peripatetic fly fishers. Because of the huge reputation of this part of the Bow though, the river above the city of Calgary has largely been ignored, at least by the general fly-fishing public. In recent years a small number of dedicated fly fishers have begun to study the upper river diligently, and they are finding it to be a fine, worthy trout stream.

The river begins north of clean, cold Bow Lake as a trickle of ice water running off the rocks into an alpine meadow in Banff National Park. The river emerges glacial blue from the lake at an elevation of 6353 feet, its pure, pristine water struggling to carry small numbers of small brook and cutthroat trout and mountain whitefish. It courses through pungent, unlogged evergreen forest, skirting Lake Louise, the most photographed spot in the Canadian Rockies and frequent site of World Cup ski races, before reaching the resort town of Banff. A short distance downstream of the town the river leaves the mountainous national park and moves toward the foothills. Pine forest gives way to mixed aspen parkland as the river winds 60 miles to the big city of Calgary, where a heritage of beef cattle, rail cars, and grain elevators has been dwarfed by a newer legacy of black gold.

Banff National Park, established in 1885, straddles the Upper Bow Corridor. Summer evenings, the towns of Banff and Canmore, just east of the park, sway to the strains of the Tourist Waltz. The dancers, most from the U.S. and Japan, are drawn by the wild beauty and natural wonders of the Canadian Rockies and by carriage-trade resorts like the Banff Springs Hotel and Chateau Lake Louise.

The upper Bow is a big river, yet it has plenty of islands and side channels that give much of it a small-stream personality. The bottom is gravel and stone, but the banks are stable and earthen, with plenty of logjams, deadfall and sweepers to provide great trout habitat.

It looks to my eye like a cutthroat stream—quick-paced, clear and sprightly, with the mountainous setting that I've come to expect from cutthroat water. And cutthroats once were the river's prime tenants, along with their nasty cousins the bull trout, but the cutts were slowly evicted by excessive angler harvest through the middle part of the 20th century. Today's main residents of the upper Bow are brown and brook trout, along with mountain whitefish and some bulls. The introduction of the browns is well documented. A hatchery truck carrying Loch Leven strain and bound for other Alberta trout streams broke an axle near the bridge over Carrot Creek, an upper Bow tributary. Rather than let the fish die the driver turned the 45,000 fry loose in the creek. This happened in 1925 and is the only recorded stocking of browns in the Bow River system. Bow Falls in the town of Banff prevents fish from moving upstream, so brown trout are not present above the falls.

There is less certainty about the arrival of the brook trout, but the accepted story is that 800 adult brookies from Ontario's Nipigon River were introduced to the upper Bow in 1904 by employees of the Canadian Pacific Railroad.

Beginning about 35 miles below Banff, the river is controlled by a series of power-producing dams that cause severe, sudden, and frequent fluctuations in river levels from the town of Seebe downstream to a re-regulation dam just west of Calgary. Such erratic flows are detrimental to fish populations. It's hard to set up housekeeping when the kitchen floods twice a day.

From the town of Banff downstream to the first power dam at Seebe, however, the river is both beautiful to look at and productive to fish. Part of the improvement at Banff is natural, as the river gains some nutrients and some temperature from hot springs that enter the river. The town also contributes some nutrients in a less natural way which increases the population of insect life in the river.

The browns have done especially well in this part of the Bow. They have taken to the upper river's abundant bankside cover like, well, like brown trout to bankside cover, and they frequently grow to impressive size.

In the pre-runoff period of April and early May, the fishing is erratic. It's possible to find Blue-winged Olives and midges hatching and fish eating them, but it's also possible to find yourself wondering why you're not skiing instead of fishing. It's not hard to do both. The ski resorts stay open into May, and you might want to ski in the morning and fish the upper Bow the same afternoon. Fishing is interrupted by runoff that generally begins in late May and lasts two or three weeks.

Prime dry-fly season is from the end of runoff until the end of September. In early fall the fishing is usually good, and it's also the prettiest time to be on the river. The fishing tails off in October when the water cools down and many of the bigger browns leave the Bow for small tributaries in preparation to spawn. The tributaries are closed to fishing in the fall.

The fish can be caught throughout the spring and summer with a variety of fly-fishing methods, but the best fishing is prompted by two major hatches that occur nearly simultaneously in midsummer. The first of these is a stonefly, but not the one you might expect. The upper Bow gets hatches of both high-profile stoneflies, the Golden Stone and the Salmonfly, but neither in enough numbers to cause much excitement. The stonefly that does produces heart palpitations in Banff and Canmore fly fishers is a size 10 brown bug, from the *Perlodidae* family called, logically enough, the Medium Brown Stone. This bug's preferred habitat is deadfall. The nymphs crawl out onto logjams to emerge and the adults stay around them until they receive the mysterious signal to mate and lay eggs. During the course of their routine, many adult stoneflies end up in the water near the deadfall and logjams.

If you see big, clumsy bugs fluttering near the water, or if you notice robins and other birds grazing daintily along the logjams, think stoneflies, rising brown trout and stout leaders. Emergence begins in early July and lasts a couple of weeks. At the peak of the hatch the fishing with chocolate brown Stimulators in size 8 and 10 is outstanding.

My first experience with these insects was in July of 1998 while filming an episode of the *Iron Blue Fly Fishing* TV series that I hosted. The water was still swollen from early summer rain and wading was difficult, at least in the places we most wanted to fish. Guide Dan Bell slid the driftboat below a big logjam, backrowed it into position and held it there with the oars so I could cast up amongst the trailing logs and debris where the fish were rising. It was tricky casting, and I developed a bit of a guilt complex as every once in awhile I'd glance over my shoulder and note the beads of sweat running down Dan's forehead as he smiled and leaned into the oars while I lost another yet fly in a log (they were his flies). Finally a good trout took way back in there, whereupon Dan heaved a sigh of relief bigger than mine, spun the boat and moved it out of the fast current into a back-eddy where we could land the fish. This was an 18-inch brown, heavy-bodied and dramatically decorated with gold flanks and orange spots. Fish like this are not unusual in the upper Bow and though they average much smaller, they are regularly taken considerably larger.

The second bug to stir fish and fishermen is the Western Green Drake, (*Drunella grandis*), a universally important western mayfly that arrives shortly after the medium brown stone. Most standard imitations in size 8 and 10 work well, but I've come to favour one I call the Crystal Green Drake, so-named because of the upright wing of crystal flash that improves the visibility of the fly on grey days. It's common to find both the full-sized Western Green Drake and its size 12 cousin (*Drunella flavilinea*) bringing

ORVIS

upper Bow browns to the surface through late August.

In September the upper river gets a size 18 or 20 Blue-winged Olive and a size 14 mayfly local anglers refer to as a Red Quill. Noticeable by its absence from the upper Bow's fall menu is good hopper fishing. This simply isn't great grasshopper habitat.

The river gets other bug activity also, but it's important to remember that this is not a spring creek or a tailwater, but a freestone mountain river, and with the exception of some evening flights of caddisflies, most hatches are sparse. But even a sparse hatch will get some upper Bow browns looking up, provided one critical condition prevails—a cloudy sky. On bright days you won't find the browns coming to the surface for any kind of hatch, but if there is heavy cloud cover they'll come from nowhere to feed on the surface even if the hatch is sparse. While filming the TV show, we spent two days on the upper river. The first was showery, dark, and cool. Stoneflies flew, fish rose, cameras whirred, and the director bought drinks later. The second was bright, warm, and clear—a perfect day for beer commercials and a lousy day to catch fish. This was the day we shot all our "pretty stuff" because the only trout seen was a gorgeous 20-inch male caught by cameraman Paul Connolly during lunch break. When the weather is bright, plan to fish well into the evening if you're set on dry-fly fishing.

The best approach on this piece of water, though, is simply not to be set on dry-fly fishing. The primary method through all seasons and between summer hatches is streamer fishing. For this a fast sinking-tip line in 6- or 7-wt is ideal, coupled with a short, stout leader you'll need for steering big fish away from the logs. Upper Bow guides favour olive or purple Crystal Buggers, and brown or green Clouser Minnows, all in size 4 and 6.

Streamers can be fished successfully with the time-honoured method of wading and working down a run, trying to swing the fly diagonally through the sweet spots. The best method, though, is from a drifting boat, which allows you to swim a streamer seductively along an undercut bank or beneath a spruce sweeper. The technique is much the same as that pioneered on Montana's Beaverhead River, where the flies are cast as close as possible to the willows that line the banks. On the Bow the targets are undercut banks, logjams and sweepers; both rivers require bold casting, hefty leaders and plenty of flies.

Dry flies can also be fished on foot or from boats. Most anglers prefer 5- or 6-wt rods that are quick enough to deliver big, bushy dries into a stiff breeze with a minimum of false casts. Fishing from a boat allows beautiful, long, drag-free drifts next to the bankside cover.

Nymph fishing is not considered a staple method by upper Bow experts. The lies favoured by the brown trout are very difficult to fish with nymphs because of all the deadfall in the water. If you try to fish nymphs there, you'll be making frequent stops at the fly shop for more ammunition. If you fish out in the riffles and runs that are clear of debris, you'll catch whitefish.

The upper Bow is not a river to compete with the Bighorn or Missouri (or the Bow near Calgary) in numbers or size of fish, but many people find fishing the upper river to be a great way to add spice to a spring ski trip, a family summer holiday in Banff, or a fishing trip to other Alberta waters. And, if you find yourself in the neighbourhood when the stoneflies and Green Drakes are hatching, the brown trout of the upper Bow can easily become the main reason for your trip. Don't be surprised if you find yourself scrapping plans to take in the Calgary Stampede or West Edmonton Mall, simply so you can get in a few more days on the beautiful and "unknown" part of the famous Bow.

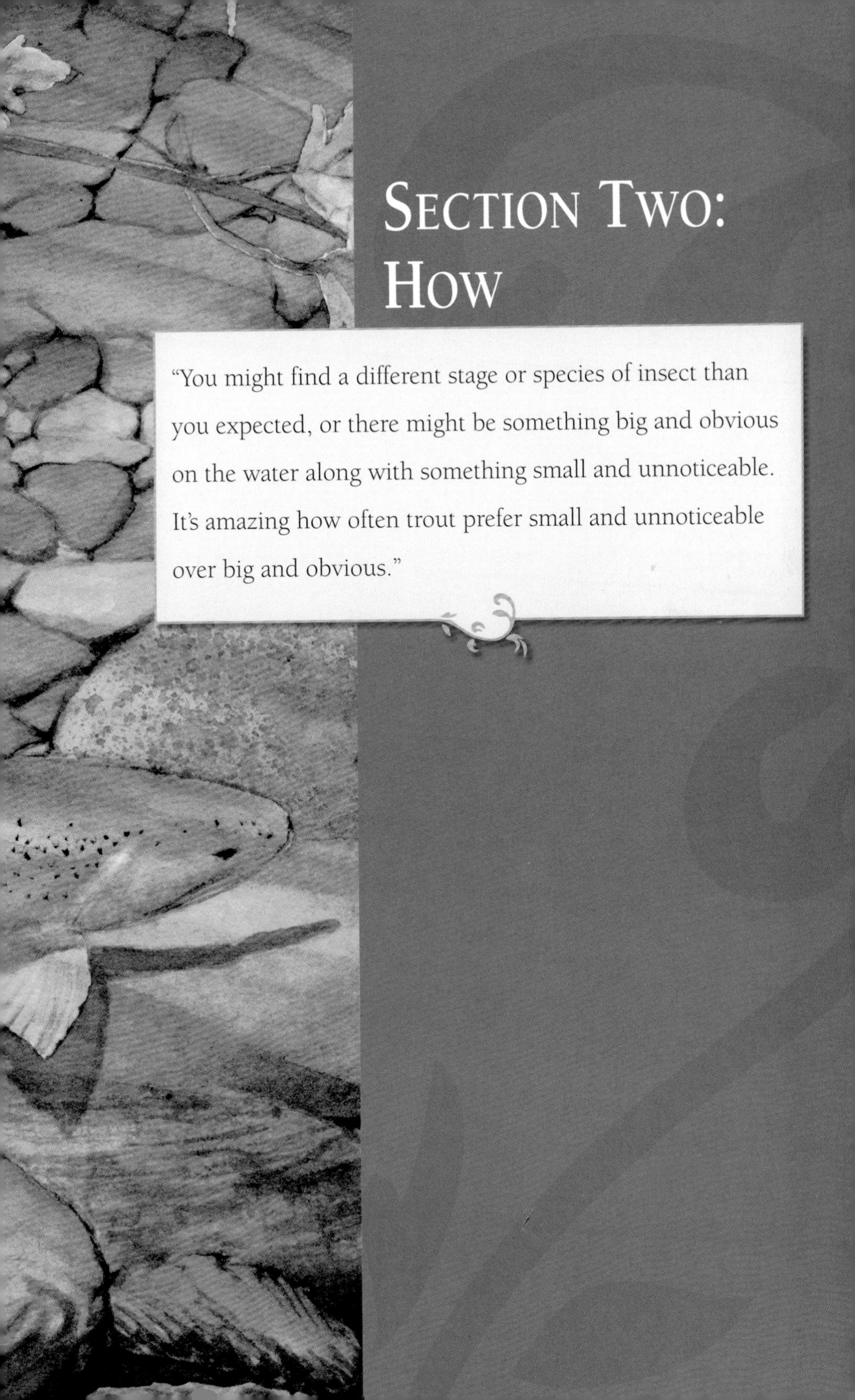

Section Two: How

"You might find a different stage or species of insect than you expected, or there might be something big and obvious on the water along with something small and unnoticeable. It's amazing how often trout prefer small and unnoticeable over big and obvious."

CHAPTER 1

Listening to the River

2007

Fly fishing is simple. All we're trying to do is imitate the fish's natural food with our artificial fly. There are three steps. First we choose a fly that represents the item the fish are currently eating. Then we put the fly in a place where the fish are eating it. Finally we make the fly behave like that natural food item. Okay, maybe simple isn't exactly the right word, because each step comes with a question: What are they eating? Where are they eating it? How does it behave? Finding and using the answers to these questions is the process of fly fishing. So where do the answers come from? These days they come from many places – books, magazines, fishing clubs, fishing friends, the Internet. There is so much information available to fly fishers today that there's no reason not to be armed with some of it when you leave home.

This pre-trip research is good and useful, but it is not listening to the river. Listening to the river begins when you are close enough to hear what it is saying. All plans and intentions should be considered starting points only. The river and the fish have the power and right to trump all plans. If the information you got from the Internet is a week old, things may have changed by the time you get to the river. Water conditions might be different or the hatch that gave the Internet reporter great fishing may now be over. Or, perish the thought, the Internet reporter may have been stretching the truth.

Observation is one of the cornerstones of fly fishing, so when you get to water you haven't seen in a while take a moment to look around. What is the water level? Is it high, low, normal? You can get this information from the Internet too, but give more credence to how the stream looks when you're standing next to it. Then, what is the water temperature? I ask this question nearly every time someone tells me about a recent fishing trip, and nearly every time they say they didn't take the water temperature. This is odd, first because water temperature is a huge factor in trout's behaviour, and second because I know these guys carry every fly-fishing gadget known to Man, including thermometers. When the water temperature is below about 4°C, trout move into slower, deeper water. When the temperature is above about 20°C, they move into faster, broken water where there is a higher level of dissolved oxygen. In the heat of summer we should fish early in the morning when the water is at its coolest, and in early spring and late fall we should fish in the afternoon when the water is at its warmest.

Also consider the clarity of both the water and the sky. Rainbow and brown trout are less nervous about being seen by predators and feed more eagerly if one or the other is cloudy. If the visibility in the water is less than a foot though, it becomes a handicap to the fly fisher.

Some of the things you observe when you're fishing are obvious – a heavy hatch of big flies, a pod of rising fish. But some are subtle. You might see a swarm of mayfly spinners dancing over a riffle, for instance. The spinners are preparing to lay eggs, after which the females will fall to the surface of the water. So swarms of spinners in the air can be a forecast of rising fish in an hour or so. Or, you see stonefly shucks on the rocks along the edge of the water. This means that both stonefly adults and nymphs are probably current trout foods. You might suddenly notice birds active at the surface of the water. Watch one bird closely. If it flies low and occasionally reaches

down to pluck something off the surface of the water, there are bugs there. If there are a lot of birds doing this - swallows or gulls most likely - it means there are a lot of bugs on the surface. Guess what other creatures might be taking advantage of a chance for an easy meal?

Noticing these kinds of things is good, but seeking them out is better. Shake a few bushes as you walk along the river and watch what falls out and flies away. Look at spider webs to see what insects are trapped there. Check the radiator of your car to see what kinds of bugs you drove through on the way to the water.

When you're near the stream, always keep one eye on the water. You might see a rise that you didn't expect. Also, learn to look through the surface and down into the water. Every now and then you'll spot a fish that you would otherwise spook. When you lay down on the bank to have a nap, keep one ear out for the sound of a rising fish.

Fly fishing's two eternal questions are "How long should I stay in one spot?" and "When should I change flies?" The short answer to both is this: If what you're doing isn't working, change something fairly quickly. That something can be the fly, the method, or the place where you're standing. Or, you can change fish by moving to a completely new spot on the stream. The worst thing to do is stand in one place for hours and repeat something that isn't working. A big part of listening to the river is realizing when it's telling you to stop doing what you're doing and try something else.

One of the most skilled fly fishers anywhere is George Anderson of Livingston, Montana. Just watching George can wear you out. He's constantly on the move and nearly always tinkering with his terminal tackle. If he's nymphing, he's adding weight, removing weight, changing flies, and changing his position. If he's fishing to rising fish he makes only three or four casts before changing the fly. George is a superb caster and reader of water, and as a result probably makes perfect presentations six times in eight casts. The rest of us need more chances so we shouldn't change as quickly as he does, but there's still a great lesson in this. If the fish doesn't take on

the first three or four perfect drifts, the next fifty or hundred won't convince it to either.

If fish are rising, but you can't fool them with an imitation of the bug you think they're eating, use a fine screen to take a sample from the surface of

the water. Catch some bugs from the same line of current the fish are feeding in and you'll get a close look at what's on the menu. This might surprise you. You might find a different stage or species of insect than you expected, or there might be something big and obvious on the water along with something small and unnoticeable. It's amazing how often trout prefer small and unnoticeable over big and obvious. Sampling the water is a simple thing, yet few fly fishers do it.

Lest you think I follow my own advice, let me tell you a little story. I fished the Missouri River earlier this summer, and the Internet reports said the caddis fishing in the evenings was exceptional. About 8:00 pm I parked the van, rigged up with a size 16 CDC Caddis and walked up the river. Sure enough there were swarms of caddis buzzing just above the water. I found a fish rising and cast the caddis over him expectantly, but with less than the desired result. I repeated this performance with numerous fish. At one point I did notice that although there were millions of caddisflies in the air, there didn't seem to be any on the water. The fish were feeding on something else, but I didn't change my fly because I was sure the trout had to start eating caddis at any moment. But they didn't. They didn't eat caddis because there were never any caddis on the water. By the time I was ready to accept this fact, it was too dark to change flies. The next day I stopped in at the fly shop in Craig and told my sad tale. "That's too bad," the guy behind the counter said. "We went out for an hour after work last night. They weren't eating caddis, but man did we kill 'em on rusty spinners." Oops. I guess I wasn't listening.

A big part of the satisfaction in fly fishing comes from solving these kinds of puzzles ("breaking the code," as I've heard it described by a fly fisher from an earlier era). It's fairly easy to learn the mechanical skills of various fly-fishing methods, but the art comes with knowing when to do what. This involves gathering information, observing circumstances, and listening to the river. A trout stream speaks quietly - often in riddles, puzzles, and rhetorical questions - but speak it does. Listen.

CHAPTER 2

Nymphing Without Indicators

2001

Nymph fishing is more popular today than ever before and most everybody who does it catches fish. The standard method on many streams calls for a Bead Head Prince Nymph or San Juan Worm with a split shot and a big fluorescent strike indicator on the leader. I think the popularity of this method is grounded in its effectiveness - and that's good. Nymphing with strike indicators provides a quick, direct route to success for new fly fishers, and who could object to that? And why would someone want to stop using a method that's so successful? Let me try to explain: I think most of us use indicators more than we need to, and I believe there are concrete reasons for fishing nymphs without them part of the time.

The use of strike indicators is not new. Early fly fishers were as capable as we are of recognizing the difficulty in detecting strikes with sunken flies and upstream casts, and one solution then as now was to attach markers to leaders. But in the old days this was one of many methods an angler might choose. Today there is an implied presumption that if you fish a nymph, you must use a strike indicator.

There are situations where you really do need to use indicators. They are essential when you can't detect a strike by feeling the fish take or by seeing your line or leader move. This is usually the case when you're making casts more than 40 feet long into water more than four feet deep. You won't feel strikes because there is too much line between you and the fly to transmit the sensation of the fish's take, and you won't see your line or leader move because they're some distance from you and the leader is entirely under water. You also need an indicator when bad light prevents you from seeing your line or leader on the water. In this instance you don't know where your fly is or how it's behaving. This happens on grey days or when you're fishing into a low sun.

But there are other circumstances where indicators are a handicap. On some heavily-fished streams the fish learn to interpret the presence of the glowing orange ball as a kind of warning and they become reluctant to feed when it's drifting repeatedly over their heads. In human terms, it's a little like learning not to pet a growling dog. After you've been bitten a few times, you don't do it anymore.

Using an indicator that's too large can sometimes cause more problems than it solves. The splat of a big corky landing on flat water can instantly clear a pool of fish. A better idea for slick water is to grease part of the leader butt with fly floatant so it will float and remain visible.

As well as being wind resistant and difficult to cast, large indicators are more susceptible to drag than smaller indicators. When the indicator starts to drag, it makes a big fuss on the surface and causes the nymph to move unnaturally under the water, both of which can spook trout. If you need to use an indicator, use the smallest, dullest-coloured one you can.

In many instances, a strike indicator also functions as a depth regulator, keeping the fly a fixed distance below the surface. This is good when the depth of the holding water is consistent. But when the depth varies greatly, as it does in areas of boulders and pocket water, it becomes a hindrance. In these places the indicator must be repositioned frequently to keep the nymph drifting at the proper depth. An indicator placement that's perfect for one spot might be completely wrong for the next spot just a short distance up the run. It's annoying to have to make adjustments every few casts, and most people don't bother to do it. Consequently, they catch fish only when their terminal rig happens to suit the specific bit of water they're casting into. The rest of the time their flies drift above the fish's heads or hang up on the stream bottom. In broken-water nymphing situations, it's more effective to fish without an indicator, simply because you can control the depth of your fly "manually" with your rod tip. You spend more time fishing and less time tinkering with all the stuff attached to your leader.

A strike indicator also functions as a velocity regulator. It drifts at the same speed as the current at the surface of the stream. This isn't necessarily good. Because of friction, the velocity at the bottom of the stream is always less than the velocity at the surface. This effect is magnified in areas where there are big rocks on the stream bottom. When your fly is near the bottom, where you generally want it to be, it should drift at the same speed as the current down there. But as your indicator drifts at "surface speed," it pulls your fly along at that speed too, which, from the fish's perspective is too fast. A leader without an indicator slices cleanly through the surface currents, allowing the nymph to drift at the proper speed near the bottom of the stream.

Indicators can also be a disadvantage when you're sight fishing to clearly visible trout. If you depend on an indicator to tell you when you've had a take, you'll miss some fish simply because your indicator won't "indicate" every take you get. This was made clear to me sight-fishing in New Zealand, where the guides use indicators partly to appease the habits of their North American clients and partly so they'll know when the fly is in the fish's vicinity. Several times the guide yelled “strike!” while I watched the indicator drift smoothly along without so much as a shudder. The guide pointed out that the indicator won't twitch or move at all if there is an excess of slack in the leader between fly and indicator when the fish takes. Neither will it twitch if a trout takes the fly while moving toward the indicator. If you can see the fish well, watch him closely and strike when he moves toward your fly or opens his mouth at the right moment.

Fishing without an indicator forces you to develop your ability to see into the water. This not only helps your nymph fishing, but is a great asset for all your fishing. It's a skill that can be enhanced with practice but is largely neglected by North American fly fishers.

Those are the concrete reasons for fishing without indicators at times. Here's the abstract reason: I believe the constant use of indicators inhibits or slows down the development of your skill. It does so by taking a three-dimensional activity and reducing it to two. When using an indicator, the angler doesn't need to worry about the depth or drift of the fly because the indicator takes care of it all for him. His concentration stops at the big orange ball - and so does his development as a nymph fisher.

This may or may not be a good analogy: strike indicators are like water wings. Water wings make swimming easier and are a great aid to the development of confidence in a new swimmer. There would be nothing wrong with using them every time you went to the beach or the pool. But, how much would you develop as a swimmer?

The best nymph fishers I know are 3-D anglers. They have a great ability

to focus on the drift of the fly and visualize what's happening under the surface, whether they're using indicators or not. Their mind's eye follows the leader right down to the bottom of the river. I'm convinced you become more adept at reading the currents and knowing what your fly is doing when you're forced to think your way to the bottom of the stream. When you catch fish this way, it translates into a greater sense of accomplishment, and consequently, more fun. And once you become confident that you can catch fish without an indicator, you'll be downright dangerous when you use one.

So when and how do you fish nymphs without an indicator? A good time is when you're fishing at close range in broken water. In choppy runs you can get quite close to the fish and you can often operate with no more than 5 to 15 feet of fly line out past the rod tip (plus a 9 or 10-foot leader). The cast is made up and across stream, so that the fly lands a few feet above the spot where you think the fish are holding. Through the drift, the rod tip is held forward and up far enough to keep all the fly line off the water. This allows a deep, slow drift of the nymph, because the fly line doesn't pull the fly along at surface speed. The rod tip moves downstream with the fly, leaving just enough slack in the system to allow a drag-free drift. There are three reference points to be aware of: the rod tip, the line/leader connection, and the point where the leader enters the water. Concentrate on the latter, and watch as far down the leader as you can see. When things are going well, you'll notice that your leader is moving downstream slightly slower than the water. This is a good sign, for it means that your fly is deep and drifting at the proper speed.

This method is best when the casting distance is less than about 25 feet. A cast beyond that leaves a few feet of fly line floating on the water, which makes strike detection slightly more difficult. Your concentration must then be focused on the end of the fly line or whatever portion of the leader you can see under the water.

With this method, strikes can usually be detected one of four ways. You might feel a short, sharp tap through your rod. It might be a rock, it might be a snag, or it might be a trout. Set the hook to find out. Second, you might see your leader twitch, slow down, or change direction in its drift. It might be a rock, it might be a snag, it might be your imagination or it might be a trout. Set the hook. Third, with your peripheral vision you might notice a sudden flash or movement deep in the water that could mean the take of a fish. Fourth, "use the force, Luke." If you think you should set the hook, do it. Don't wait until you can explain to yourself why you think you should do it. You'll be surprised sometimes to find you've hooked a fish and yet have no idea why you struck. This is okay. In fact, it's great. It means you're learning to detect the subtlest of messages. And when it happens, pretend you planned it that way, especially if other fishermen are watching. When I'm teaching this short-line nymphing method, I often tell the students, "Find a reason to set the hook sometime during this drift." This helps them to intensify their concentration and to expect a strike instead of being surprised by a strike.

The two best nymph fishermen I've fished with are George Anderson of Livingston, Montana, and Jim Gilson from central Pennsylvania. Though there are some differences in their techniques, they share a remarkable ability of knowing when a fish has taken the fly. I've stood beside them both, watching, and it's often impossible to know what message they've received that tells them to strike. All I'm certain of is that they make it look very easy – short cast, short drift, quick strike, fish on.

I want to make it clear that I don't consider the use of indicators to be an ethical issue. There is nothing wrong with using them for all your nymph fishing; the fish don't really care. The most difficult part of nymphing without an indicator is convincing yourself to try it. Here's my advice: Next time you're in some broken water and the nymphing is hot, live on the edge—take your corky off. Think your way down the leader to the fish by using the force, ditching the water wings, and working without a net—and without an indicator.

CHAPTER 3

Low Water, Large Trout

2006

Many fly fishers feel great affection for late season. They like the way trout streams and their surroundings look, feel, and smell in the perfect days of autumn. The weather is generally good, the water conditions are good, and the river valleys are saturated with colour. I count myself among this group of fly fishers who are obsessed with September and October, but in truth much of our affection comes because of the sensory impact of the season, not because the fish are particularly co-operative. In fact the trout – especially the big trout – are generally harder to catch in the low, clear water conditions that come with fall.

To understand why, we must consider the two defense instincts trout use to foil anglers. The first is simply that they are wild animals, and as such, the need for safety trumps all other needs, including the need for food. Have you ever seen a rising fish spooked by a swallow flying over the water? A fish loses his appetite the instant it senses danger or even the possibility of danger. They are extremely wary and always on the lookout for signs of trouble.

The trout's second defense is their ability to feed with great discrimination, carefully inspecting each potential food item before eating it. This trait develops most intensely where there is heavy catch-and-release fishing pressure. After the fish have been "burned" a few times by artificial flies, they get harder and harder to fool.

What's interesting about these two defenses is that they operate on a continuum and offset each other. At one end of the scale are wilderness trout that have never encountered an angler. These fish are usually very easy to fool, but also very skittish and difficult to approach. The angler's biggest challenge is getting the fly in front of the fish without scaring them first. If he succeeds at that, the fish will probably take most any fly. But if he fails and frightens the fish, they might not feed again that day.

At the opposite end of the continuum are the highly sophisticated trout of heavily fished waters. On streams like Armstrong and Nelson's spring creeks in Montana, the trout are fished over every day. These fish learn to feed in the presence of anglers, simply because they have no other choice. They're not much bothered by wading fishermen or by false casts shooting over their heads. They'll stop feeding when they see them but will be back at it in just a few minutes. Their defense is not to flee but rather to become more careful about what they eat. Such fish are easy to approach but very difficult to fool.

There are, of course, many fish that rest somewhere near the middle of the continuum, exhibiting a blend of the skittish behaviour of wilderness trout and the selective behaviour of "educated" trout.

No matter what kind of stream you fish, the playing field is severely tilted in the fish's favour by late summer. The water in back country streams is lower and clearer than any other time, which makes the trout harder than ever to approach. The trout in heavily-fished streams are in full-selective mode, having had a whole season to develop their skepticism for artificial flies. And naturally it's the biggest fish that take best advantage of their instincts. Autumn trout can drive you crazy, but here are a few ideas to help you overcome the handicaps and catch big fish in low water.

Watch the Weather

It's always best to fish for trout that are either feeding or ready to feed, and different species of fish are active in different kinds of weather. For example, on bright, warm days, think cutthroats; that's the weather they favour. In September and October, the water in high country cutthroat streams remains cold until midday, and most insect and fish activity occurs around mid afternoon.

If the day is dark and gloomy however, it could be a great day to look for a big rainbow or brown. Work the water with streamers and nymphs in the morning, but stay on the lookout for rising fish, because dark, damp fall weather usually brings on afternoon hatches of Blue-winged Olive mayflies. Though these flies are small, they emerge in great numbers and are the best hatch for bringing the big fish to the surface in the fall.

Emulate Elmer and the Kiwis

The best philosophy on approaching trout in low water comes from the fly-fishing guides of New Zealand and is summarized succinctly by Elmer Fudd: We must be vewy, vewy quiet. Those guys (the Kiwi guides, not Elmer) earn their living by spotting, approaching, and helping people catch wild brown trout in the clearest of water, so there's value in paying attention to how they do it.

The most important rule is to do everything you can to avoid alerting the fish to your presence before you start casting. This is always important but is more difficult to achieve in low water when the fish can see you easily.

Approach the water slowly and cautiously. Look for signs of fish's presence before you barge in and start casting. Stay farther from the fish than you would earlier in the season and avoid false casting over fish in shallow water. Wear dull-coloured clothing that doesn't reflect a lot of light, and avoid silhouetting your profile so the fish can see it.

Fish With Finesse

The over-riding theme in fishing in low, clear water is to increase finesse and delicacy in every way, including the tackle you choose. Use 3- or 4-wt fly lines in small streams and 4- or 5-wts in bigger water. If you use a 9-foot leader on a particular stream in July, a 12-footer will be better in September. You might also use a tippet that's one size lighter and made of fluorocarbon. Fluorocarbon reflects less light in the water and is less visible to trout. The flies should probably be smaller as well, both because most natural insects are smaller in the fall, and because a smaller fly is less likely to spook a fish when it arrives on his dinner table.

The need for delicacy doesn't only apply to dry-fly fishing, but is also necessary when you're fishing nymphs in low water. In early summer your terminal nymphing tackle might consist of a couple of size 4 stonefly nymphs, two big split shot, and an indicator the size of a ping-pong ball. It might be fine in June when the water is higher, but this kind of a rig will send fish scurrying for cover in September. In the fall use smaller nymphs, longer, finer leaders, less weight, and a less obtrusive indicator. You can also go radical and use a nymph that isn't a bead-head. In most places bead-heads are hugely popular, which means you might gain some points with the trout by showing them an old fashioned "beadless" nymph. A great universal fall nymph is a Pheasant Tail in size 16 or 18.

Break Some Rules

In some streams the fish rise reliably to daily afternoon hatches of *Baetis* or *Pseudocloeon* mayflies in the fall. That's the good news. The bad news is that these are often the most frustrating fish of the season. They are intimidating trout, rising repeatedly in clear view, yet seemingly incapable of making the mistake you're waiting for. I'm thinking of the Missouri River in Montana and the Crowsnest River in southwestern Alberta now, but it happens in many places throughout North America.

You'll probably go through several fly changes in one of these hatches, and you might find a fly that works. But if you don't, consider changing your method. If the water is slow and flat, try the unconventional approach of fishing downstream to the rising fish. This method developed on hard-fished waters like Idaho's Henry's Fork of the Snake, where the trout all have PhDs in Selectivity. By delivering the fly from a position up and across from the fish, you show the trout the fly before you show him the leader, and this goes a long ways toward fooling a large, finicky feeder. To do it you must first position yourself far enough from the fish that he doesn't see you. Then deliver the fly to a spot a few feet above the trout with an upstream reach cast. As the fly drifts down over the fish, move the rod downstream at the same speed as the current. This gives you a fly-first, drag-free drift. You'll

have some reduction in hooking success with this method because the striking motion pulls the fly away from the fish's mouth, but you'll get far more takes this way.

Remember Your Favourite Ant

Most fly fishers know that late summer is a good time to fish with terrestrials, but many of them don't use any terrestrials except grasshoppers. There are other land-borne bugs that are important to trout, and the most common of these are ants. An ant is a good searching pattern anytime from August through October. Though it seems to defy logic, trout sometimes favour ants over bigger bugs, even grasshoppers. This was proven to me by some brown trout on an Alberta stream one September day many years ago. At the suggestion of my host, I fished with two dry flies together – a size 6 Dave's Hopper and a size 16 Black Ant. There weren't many fish caught, but they were all good-sized, and every one took the small ant over the juicy hopper that drifted just a few inches away. To find the ant connoisseurs in your favourite stream, concentrate on good holding water near the shoreline, particularly along grassy, undercut banks. Use a black or rusty brown ant in size 14, 16, or 18. These flies can be hard to see on the water, so you might want to pair the ant with a large, visible dry fly, or attach a small, bright piece of yarn to the tippet about 12 inches from the fly.

One of the best events of the fall fly-fishing season is called an "ant fall," when hundreds of flying ants suddenly end up on the water. Nobody seems to know why this happens, nor how to predict when it will happen, but when it does the trout almost always respond by feeding heavily. It seems to be a one-day event, almost always occurring randomly sometime in September. An ant fall is not something you can pursue the way you can a salmonfly or Green Drake hatch, but if you spend enough time on enough streams in September you'll stumble across it and when you do, you'll like it.

CHAPTER 4

Nice Fish, Dad

1995

The other day my eight year-old daughter announced that she wanted to take her fly rod to school for show and tell. One of the greatest privileges of my life has been watching this child grow up, and I don't need to tell you how it pleases me that she wants to learn to fish with a fly rod.

Kids often start fishing with spin or spin-casting tackle because they can learn to cast easily, but if the adult is using a fly rod the child will eventually notice the difference and want to do it that way too.

At this point most kids are happy to leave you in charge of the casting and hooking of fish with the fly rod if they can reel them in. But before long that won't be good enough and they'll want to do it "all by themselves," including the casting. That's your cue to get them their own outfit and show them how to use it.

About this time many youngsters go through a period of frustration because their desire to fly-cast has arrived, but their strength and physical coordination haven't. It's the parent's job to smooth out these rough spots, and one thing that helped in our case was to offer our daughter the job of netting our fish. She liked this, and it made up a little for her frustration with casting. The good news is that this difficult period doesn't last long and with some basic instruction and a proper outfit most kids can be through it and casting quite nicely on their own by the time they're about ten years old.

A good outfit for a child is a 4- or 5-wt weight rod between seven and eight feet long. My daughter's rod is an eight footer for a 4-wt line, but she uses a 5-wt on it. I recommend over-lining by one size because the heavier line helps load the rod on a short cast and allows the child to feel the rod bending at the beginning of the cast.

You can begin teaching casting in the backyard. It's unlikely you have a prodigy so keep the sessions short, be patient and encouraging, and don't expect miracles. Try and cast with the child a couple of times a week for a month or so before heading for the water.

Where and how you take your children fishing is critical. Don't just try to work them in on one of your regular weekend trips with the rest of the guys. Nobody wins at that game. Instead plan special outings to places that suit kids – places easy to get to, where the casts can be short and the fish are plentiful. Youngsters don't care about how big the fish are, so aim for numbers rather than size. It's best to have kids start by fishing from their feet rather than from a boat, so find a farm pond stocked with trout or perch, or look for a small creek that has backcast room and lots of little brook trout or cutthroats.

Keep the outings short and encourage the kids to do other things if they want to, like throwing rocks in the water or reading a book. Your objectives are clear and simple – to make sure the kids have fun on the outing and to make sure they want to do it again.

One other thing: don't forget the camera. You'll both want to record that first fish.

The clock is ticking and I'm reminded daily of how limited our time with our children is. Teach them to fish with you now and you're laying the foundation for something you'll both have forever.

CHAPTER 5

Handling Drag

1985

I crawled under some willows for shelter from the rain. One of those brief, but heavy sun showers had enveloped an Alberta spring creek in the middle of a gorgeous June afternoon. While huddled under the trees, I caught a glint out of the corner of my eye. A good-size trout had started sipping flies in a tiny bay along the far bank under a low overhanging willow branch. When I couldn't stand watching him any longer, I crept into position to cast.

The shower made it impossible to see the little Blue-winged Olive I was fishing. I made several dozen casts that seemed about right but resulted in no takes. Eventually, the fish just quit feeding, the sun came out and I moved on.

On my next visit to the stream, I made a point of checking the same spot. With better light conditions, I could easily see the problem. It was one of those Catch-22 lies where you need a slack cast to get a drag-free float but where there's not enough space to make a slack cast. If the fly was dropped in the right place with a conventional cast, it started to drag almost before it hit the water.

As usual the solution surfaced several months later. A friend and I found some large fish rising gently along the bank of a big river. The fish were so close to the bank that they were out of the current flow. My friend made several good pitches to them, but when the fly moved nicely down the current edge, the fish wouldn't move out for it. If he put the fly in front of the fish in the still water, even with a good slack cast, drag occurred before the lazily rising fish would take it. After a few minutes, I reluctantly took my turn with these finicky risers. I could see that I wasn't about to make a better conventional presentation than my friend had, so I tried something silly. I cast a large Letort Hopper so it landed with a splat several inches above the fish in the still water. There was no time for the fish to even consider drag - he had the fly the instant it hit the water.

This may be an extreme case, but it's a good example of the "if you can't beat it, use it" method of dealing with drag. By using flies like caddis or hoppers, which may excite the fish and/or benefit from a little well-timed drag, you can sometimes provoke a take. It would have been worth a try on the spring creek if I had thought of it.

Slack Casts

Often the most useful way of dealing with drag is to try to delay it until after the fly has drifted past the fish or the expected lie of a fish, through use of one of several slack casts. A slack cast simply presents the line and leader in something other than a straight line, usually a wavy pattern. The waves in the leader dissipate under the pull of the current while the fly continues to drift naturally. The most common of these deliveries is called the S-Cast or serpentine cast. Simply wiggle the rod tip back and forth horizontally as the line settles to the water. It's easy, but in my experience not terribly effective. For a slack cast to be useful, the slack must be in the leader and the S-Cast puts slack in the line. Here are a few casts that put slack in the leader.

Dump Cast—I'm not an advocate of titles for everything, but my two favourite slack casts are ones I'll refer to as the dump cast and the tug cast. The dump cast is a funny-looking cast that, if done properly, can drop an entire 12-foot leader into a hula-hoop. On the forward cast an arcing hand motion is used to create a wide, high loop. Near the end of the cast the leader and forward part of the line hang vertically above the water. The leader and fly will drop straight down, resulting in a lot of slack, almost all of which is in the leader. The fly lands fairly close to the end of the line, but the enormous amount of slack produced allows you to drop the fly a safe distance above the fish. The drawback to the dump cast is that it's difficult to execute in wind because the high, slow delivery gives the breeze a lot of time to blow the fly off target. The cast also settles too slowly to be effective in fast water because the slack is pulled from the leader by the current before the fly lands. But when the fish are rising in slow water, it is the best way I know to put slack in the leader.

Tug Cast—The tug cast puts slack in the leader in breezy conditions or in tight casting quarters where a high, wide forward loop is impossible. Cast low to the water with more line than necessary to reach the target. The moment the line and leader are laying horizontally over the water, make a quick tug with your line hand. This makes the fly jump back toward you before it settles, leaving slack in the leader. It works on the same principle as the more common method of casting high and hard and stopping the rod abruptly to let the fly bounce back. The tug cast is more accurate, and works well in cramped quarters because it uses a tight loop that is delivered low to the water. It does not, however, provide as much slack as the dump cast.

Pocket Water Pile Cast—Another useful cast for putting slack into the leader in fast water is made by driving the fly at the surface so it hits the water before the leader unrolls, leaving the fly and leader in a mess near the end of the line. It lands too hard for use in flat water and gets no points for artistic impression, but in fast pocket water it works.

Mending

Mending adjusts the configuration of the line after it has landed on the water and is used by dry-fly fishers to increase the length of drag-free floats. Mends are often used for fishing across stream where there is faster water between

the fish and fisherman. A perfect mend flips a loop of fly line upstream without moving the fly itself, but if the mend isn't perfect one of two bad things usually happens. Sometimes the mend jerks the fly violently and spooks the fish. Other times the fly doesn't jerk, but the mend removes the slack from the leader, letting the fly drag anyway.

A mend can be used effectively on rising fish if you remember three things. First, decide if a mend will be required. Estimate what the currents will do to the line and fly before making the cast. Second, a good slack cast is essential prior to the mend, for even the best mend will remove some of the slack from the leader. If there is plenty of slack to start with, a good mend will leave enough slack to still be effective. Third, if a mend is needed, don't wait until the last minute to make it. Make the mend immediately after the fly lands, while there is still an abundance of slack in the leader. Mending is easier when the fly line is floating well, and all fly lines float best when they are clean.

Leaders

Chances of making a good slack cast with any method are improved by using a long tippet. A three-foot or longer tippet won't straighten completely but will fall to the water in waves. Lefty Kreh believes that tippet length is as important as fly pattern when fishing to rising fish. If he gets some refusals, his first assumption is that the leader or tippet isn't right. Most often this means that it isn't long enough, and consequently, isn't providing the slack necessary to get a completely drag-free float. It's also easier to make a slack cast if you use a heavily-hackled fly, because it resists moving through the air and doesn't allow the leader to straighten all the way out.

Applied Tactics

It's very difficult to get a good drag-free drift when you're fishing upstream into the tail of a pool from the riffle below. The water where the fly lands moves much slower than the water downstream where the belly of the fly line lands. In this situation, you need slack in the belly of the line as well as in the leader. A dump cast followed by several side to side waggles of the rod tip as the line settles (like the "S" cast) gives the necessary slack in these situations.

The first expert dry-fly fisherman I fished with taught me a valuable lesson with his first cast over a large rainbow that was rising in slow, flat water. My companion surprised me completely by dropping the fly about 12 inches above the fish, not five or six feet above the fish as I had been trying to do. I thought that he misjudged his cast and had made a mistake—until the fish took the fly. My friend doesn't worry about slack casts or curve casts or mending very often because he drops the fly very close to the fish and only needs a short drift. He fishes a light line with a long leader, and the small amount of slack allows the fly to drift past the fish before it starts to drag. He is good at this but it takes accurate, consistent casting and leaves no room for error. A poor fly presentation is not a problem if it occurs a few feet above the fish, but if it happens a few inches from the fish it's sure to spook him. This short-drift method also allows you to get a number of drifts over a fish in a short time, thereby increasing the time your fly is on the water in front of the fish.

While mulling a particular fishing situation over, you might realize that simply moving a step or two one way or the other before casting will put you in a better position for a good float. If that's the case you won't need to use any of these elaborate casts and mending gyrations. That would be the best tactic of all.

CHAPTER 6

Do Little Fly Rods Kill Fish?

1996

As fly fishing enjoys an unprecedented boom in popularity, more and more money is being spent by manufacturers on the development of new tackle. It seems this growth is headed two directions. Saltwater fishermen are trying to catch more and bigger species of fish with fly rods, and the tackle companies are doing their part by producing rods and reels that might slow down a submarine. At the other end of the spectrum, trout fishermen are using smaller and smaller flies as time goes by. Twenty years ago a #12 was probably average for dry flies and a #18 was considered miniscule. In the years before graphite, the smaller bugs would have been fished on a 5- or 6-wt cane or fiberglass rod, and it would have been difficult to land a three-pound fish on 5X tippet that tested only a pound or two breaking strength. Recent advances in rod materials, hooks, and leaders have pushed the boundary of the light end of our sport. Today I'd guess a #16 dry fly is about average, and the guys who are really into this small fly business don't consider a # 24 unusual.

One of the more controversial of these recent developments in tackle is the introduction of rods designed to cast extremely light fly lines. In the early 1980s, the first 3-wt rod was unveiled, and a few years later Orvis introduced the first 2-wt. Lots of fly fishers thought it was a gimmick at first and most other rod manufacturers did too, I think. There seem to have been some converts, though, because now Loomis, Sage, Scott and just about anybody who's anybody in the fly-rod business is making a 2-wt, and I'm told they're selling tons of them.

Some fishermen feel these little rods offer concrete advantages in certain fishing situations while others still think they're silly novelty items – but that's not what I'm going to talk about here.

Shortly after these light-line rods arrived on the scene, I began to hear people question the ability of these rods to handle fish once they were hooked. When *Fly Fisherman* magazine published an article comparing the various 2-wt rods, an angler from Washington state wrote a letter to the editor expressing concern that these rods were not capable of playing fish properly. He felt that a fish landed on a 2-wt rod would not recover when released because it would have been played too long.

I heard these things at a time when I was doing a lot of my fishing with 2- and 3-wts. Because I pride myself in doing whatever it takes to ensure that the fish survive my intrusion into their routine, I wondered why I hadn't noticed this problem. I had a hunch about what was going on, but I decided to get semi-scientific about it.

One day in late June, I borrowed a new 1-wt rod from a fly shop and took it out on the Bow River. I was hoping to find a good-sized fish for my experiment. As it turned out several decent fish volunteered their services, but right at dark one really caught my eye. This one was sipping spent caddisflies in the shallows right against the bank and even his slow, gentle rises pushed a lot of water out of the way. He eventually took my Elk Hair Caddis with a little slurp and then things got interesting. He bolted hard for deeper water when the hook stuck him, and then settled into the regular routine of running, jumping and head-shaking. It was awhile before I remembered that this was supposed to be an experiment, but I eventually calmed down some and tried to note what the little rod was doing.

When the fish stopped to rest, initially I tried to pressure him by raising the rod tip. The rod bent very easily right down into the grip, but the fish didn't move. But when I put the rod tip fairly low to the water and kept a small bend in the rod, the fish moved quite easily when I reeled in line. By playing the fish this way, I landed him at least as quickly as I would have with a more conventional 5- or 6-wt outfit. This was a 23-inch brown, and I mention this not because it was a wonderful achievement on my part but because it convinced me of the ability of these little rods to handle big fish.

The key is in how you use the rod. If you use it like a lever you can bend it until the butt points directly away from the fish and you still won't be able to move him. This is what leads some people to the conclusion that the rod will break before the fish moves – and it probably will if used in this manner.

If, however, you keep a relatively slight bend in the rod (with an angle of about 90 degrees between the butt of the rod and the line coming out the tip), and maintain that bend while playing the fish, everything will be fine. It's pretty logical really; if you hold the rod this way and crank on the reel, something has to happen. Either the fish will move or the tippet will break, and that's exactly the way things are supposed to be. You play the fish from the reel while keeping a slight bend in the rod to absorb the shock of the fish's fight.

Later, to further check my theory under a more controlled situation I got out 2-wt, 6-wt and 9-wt rods, put reels on them and took them into my basement. I tied the leaders to one of my heavy hunting boots and tried to drag the boot across the floor with each rod. If I tried to use the rod as a lever, the 2-wt bent severely without moving the boot. But when I kept the rod low and cranked on the reel, it made no difference which rod I used – the boot moved.

Here's the real interesting part. I think these rods may give you an advantage when playing big fish. When I was fighting the big brown with the 1-wt, a couple of times he interrupted my pulls with violent headshakes that would usually snap a fine tippet. But the little rod flexed to absorb this shock and the leader held. I know a 6-wt rod would not have absorbed this extra shock and the fish would have broken the tippet. One of the reasons I landed this fish so quickly was because I didn't have to "baby" the tippet as much as I would have with a bigger, stiffer rod. In short, I found I could put as much pressure on the fish as I thought the tippet could withstand and the rod took over from there to absorb considerably more shock when the fish bolted suddenly or shook his head. I was using 5X tippet and I don't think I could have broken it without pointing the rod directly at the fish.

I found I wasn't alone in this conclusion when I mentioned it to a friend who regularly fishes the Frying Pan River in Colorado. This is a unique stream that has fast rocky water and big fish that want small flies. The guides insist on using 1- and 2-wt rods because they are the only rods that can handle the two to six-pound fish while protecting the 5X and 6X tippets that are needed to fool the fish.

The guy who wrote to the magazine said, "If you don't want to break a rod or a tippet, you will play a fish until it is nettable, and with a 2-wt rod that means when it is dead or at least beyond resuscitation." I admire his concern, but if you understand how to use your tackle the only thing that will make you play a fish too long is using a tippet too light for the job, and that will happen no matter what rod it is attached to. Fly-fishing guru Gary Borger agrees, advising fly fishers to use the lightest fly line and the heaviest tippet they can in each fishing situation.

This is not meant to squelch debate over whether or not these light-line rods are necessary for our fishing, for that will always depend on the specific situation and the fishermen's preferences, but in my mind there is no debate about the well-being of the fish.

CHAPTER 7

Driftboat Streamer Fishing

2006

Perspective is skewed the first time you plant yourself in a boat with intentions of fly fishing while drifting down a river. The tables have been turned, and instead of watching the conveyor belt of current as it moves past you, you're on that conveyor belt, watching the banks and the lies of the fish as you move past them. After equilibrium returns, many people's first thought is, "What a great way to fish a dry fly. I can get a drag-free drift of a hundred feet." They're right, of course, and soon after this revelation comes another - that it's also a great way to fish a nymph, for the same reason.

Perhaps the strength of this dead-drift enlightenment is the reason many people never get around to fishing streamers from a drifting boat. Anglers do so at their peril though, for streamers work very well from a drifting boat. They work because they can be presented in places wading anglers can't reach and moved in directions wading anglers can't duplicate. Think of those deep outside bends overgrown with trees and brush, or all the depressions and current seams that are just out of casting range when you're wade-fishing.

You can drift a trout river in anything from a clunky rowboat to a sleek jet-sled, but most fly fishers use McKenzie-style driftboats, inflatable rafts, or pontoon boats. The techniques described here are effective from all of these but in each case the speed and position of the boat are crucial. With a raft or driftboat, these are the responsibility of the oarsman, but with a pontoon boat, it's a do-it-yourself project because you're fishing with your hands while steering with your feet. This is certified multi-tasking, but it does reduce arguments about where the boat should be positioned.

Tackle

A rod for driftboat streamer fishing needs the backbone to pick up a sinking-tip line and a heavy fly and return them to the water with a minimum of false casts. Most experts prefer a nine-foot rod for a 6- or 7-wt line.

The reel should have a smooth drag and carry at least 50 yards of backing. One of the problems with fly fishing from a boat is controlling the line that accumulates as you retrieve it. It frequently tangles around stuff in the boat, often just after you've hooked a big trout. Large arbor reels have a high-

retrieve rate that puts slack line back on the reel quickly after you've hooked up. They also help when you hook a big fish that makes an initial run upstream but then stops and comes back toward you.

The fly line should be a weight-forward taper, either a full-floating or a sinking-tip with 10 to 15 feet of type IV or V sinking line on the front. Sinking-tips are best in water that is deeper than three feet because they keep the flies closer to the bottom during the retrieve. Many anglers use sinking-tips in early summer while the rivers are receding from runoff, and switch to full-floating lines for the low, clear conditions of mid-summer and fall. All the methods described here are effective with both types of lines.

With full-floating lines nine-foot leaders are perfect, but with sinking-tip lines three to six-foot leaders keep the fly deeper in the water. Tippets should be stout - 0X, 1X or 2X - to withstand vicious strikes from big trout. The increased abrasion-resistance of fluorocarbon is a benefit in streams with sharp or jagged rocks.

In especially deep or fast water, additional weight can be added to the leader (as long as it's legal where you're fishing). Split shot or sink-putty can be placed a few inches above the fly or right against the head of the fly. I prefer the latter because it imparts a seductive up-and-down motion to the fly as it's retrieved.

Flies

This is simple. A driftboat streamer should cast easily, sink quickly, and move well in the water. If you carry nothing but various members of the Woolly Bugger family you'll be ready. Other good choices are the Clouser Minnow and Gartside Leech. Be sure to have both light and dark-coloured patterns in sizes 4, 6, and 8. Though rabbit-strip streamers have great natural action, they're not my favourites for driftboat-fishing because they hold water and cast like wet socks.

It's fun to fish two streamers together, pairing a dark one with a light one, or a large one with a small one. Attach the second fly with an additional piece of tippet tied to the bend of the first fly. Remember that it's more difficult to cast two flies because the extra weight and air-resistance slows everything down during the cast.

Bombing the Banks

If there's a traditional way to fish streamers from a drifting boat, this is it. It's also the most physically-demanding trout fishing I know of, requiring a powerful rod, a big, heavy fly (or maybe two), and lots of energy from the angler.

It is well suited to larger western rivers like the lower Henry's Fork, Clark Fork, Yellowstone, and Bow. It can be used on smaller rivers like the Beaverhead too, but on narrow streams with heavy vegetation the trees behind can interrupt a lot of backcasts.

Bombing the banks works any time of year as long as the fish are there, but the primest of prime time is while the river is receding and clearing from spring runoff. Once the water has cleared from opaque chocolate brown to foggy green with 18 inches of visibility, it's ready. The water is still high and moving quickly, but the combination of high velocity and coloured water is a bank-bomber's blessing. The high velocity moves fish to the banks and out of the heaviest flows while the cloudy water inspires them to feed more boldly with less fear of being seen by predators.

Through the heart of summer when the flow rates are lower and the water is clearer the fish may move off the banks during the day but return to them at night. In this case, try an early morning float so you can get to the trout before they retreat to deeper water. If you don't like to get up that early you can fish late into the evening with dry flies and then pound the banks with streamers as you float to the takeout at or after dusk. If there are brown trout in the river, these low-light periods are the best times to get them.

A classic piece of "bombable" water is two-feet deep or deeper near the bank and flows at medium to quick velocity. It has good structure in the form of boulders, deadfall, deflections, or beaver lodges that block or constrict current and create current seams. The greatest concentrations of this water are along the outsides of bends where current flow is strongest.

The boat should be positioned 30 to 50 feet off the bank, and slowed so that it moves about half the speed of the current. Cast at a slight downstream angle into the quiet water near the bank. If there is a current seam near the bank, cast the fly beyond the seam. Use an upstream reach cast as you deliver the fly, or make a big upstream mend as soon as the fly lands to keep the streamer pointed and moving across or slightly upstream rather than racing downstream faster than the current. If the holding water is more than three feet deep, pause briefly after mending to allow the fly to sink. Retrieve the fly so it swims out away from the bank and across the current seam.

During the retrieve it's critical to keep the rod tip low so each strip of the fly line translates into movement of the fly. Keep the rod tip just above the water and follow the streamer as it moves downstream of the boat.

Introduce additional mends each time a bow forms in the line. Try to keep the line as straight as possible between the rod tip and the fly.

In fast water where the targets are pockets near the bank, retrieve the fly just a short distance before re-casting. Three or four strips on the line are enough, for the fish usually won't chase a streamer out into the heavy current. In slower water fish will sometimes follow considerable distance, so it's best to keep retrieving until you can see the fly. Vary the retrieves to see what turns the fish on. They won't always respond to the same type of retrieve. Try long, short, quick, and slow strips, mixed with tantalizing twitches of the rod tip. When you have a strike, try to remember what you were doing so you can do it again.

Doing the Dance

A variation on bombing the banks is useful where the water is slow to medium-speed at the bank but significantly faster between the bank and the boat. Areas with good depth and lots of deadfall or boulders along the shore are ideal. Again the boat should be slowed, but in this case it should be positioned just two to three rod-lengths from the bank. Cast straight across into the quiet water near the bank, but instead of retrieving the fly by stripping the line, simply raise and twitch the rod tip to make the fly dance back toward the boat a few feet. After the fly has moved out to the edge of the faster water, make a single backcast and deliver the fly back to the bank again without false-casting. The process is simple and repetitive: Cast, twitch, twitch, twitch. Cast, twitch, twitch, twitch. It's a rapid-fire method that allows nearly every inch of bank water to be covered. It's important that the boat be kept both close to the bank and a constant distance from the bank so the fisherman doesn't have to change the length of his cast. This method is very entertaining because the strikes are always violent and usually visible. It works best during low light conditions with rubber-legged flies like the Rubber-Legged Bow River Bugger.

Slow and Deep

Trout move away from the banks when the water is excessively low, warm, or cold, and when the weather is excessively bright. Heavy driftboat pressure can also chase them to deeper water. Under these conditions when the fish are holding off the banks in deeper current seams this method, developed by Alberta guides George McBride and Eric Grinnell, often gets them.

The anglers' focus is still toward the edge of the river, but the approach is different. The boat should be positioned 30 feet or so outside of the edge of the deeper water, and slowed to half the speed of the current. After the boat has moved just downstream of the head of a current seam, cast upstream at a 45 degree angle to the top of the seam. As soon as the fly lands make an upstream mend. With the rod tip low follow the drift of the fly as it moves downstream. Retrieve with slow strips to stay in touch with the fly, and make additional mends to keep the fly moving slowly and deeply as it gradually catches up to the boat and passes it. The drift is finished when the line comes tight downstream of the boat. This method causes the fly to move slowly right along the current seam deep in the water column. Think of this method as "not quite a dead drift." The strikes are usually not violent and when a fish takes it will often seem that the fly has simply stopped drifting. Because of the depth of the water, this method works best with a sinking-tip fly line.

Synchronicity

No matter which method is being used, if two people are fishing they must keep their casts more or less parallel to avoid tangles. Murphy's Law of Driftboat Fishing says that the worst tangles will appear just as the boat approaches the best water. Two-rod tangles usually occur when the guy in the front of the boat yields to temptation and casts into a good pocket more than once. When he hits it for the third time, he's reaching back upstream and encroaching on his partner's territory. It's best to look ahead to the next good spot rather than looking back to the previous one.

Playing and Landing Fish

You can land and release trout less than 16 inches long without touching them or removing them from the water. Bring them to the boat quickly (your stout tippet will allow that) and either use a Ketchum Release Tool or simply slide your hand down to the fly, turn it upside down and give a slight shake. The fish will come off easily, especially if the hook is barbless.

The fish you're really after - the big guys - require some additional thought. If the fish is hooked in slow water, it's often best to move to shore immediately so you can get out of the boat and play the fish from your feet. If the fish is hooked in fast water however, this can be precisely the wrong thing to do. You'll wind up either chasing the fish down the bank on foot or scrambling to get back into the boat and going after him. In fast water the best plan is to fight the fish from the boat until you drift into slower water. Then you can move to shore where you or your companion can get out of the boat and land the fish.

When a fish is hooked off a deep high bank along the outside of a bend, it's often best to move the boat directly across the river to the slow, shallow water on the opposite bank. Stop and land the fish there, and then move the boat back to the good bank and resume fishing. That way you don't "waste" good water by playing a fish while floating through it.

If you're required by law or circumstance to land a big fish from the boat, use a long-handled landing net with a non-abrasive bag. Net the fish quickly, leave the fish in the net while the hook is removed, and use the net to keep the fish under control while he regains his strength.

Streamer fishing has long been known as a ticket to big fish, and if you try it the next time you float your favourite river, you might be able to prove it.

CHAPTER 8

Shallow Water Nymphing

1993

There's a primitive, visceral appeal to fooling a big fish in shallow water. It's like catching somebody with his hand in the cookie jar. For our purposes "shallow" means water less than two feet deep, and we might start by asking why a big trout would be in such skinny water. The answer is simple. He's there to eat.

It may seem odd that fish would move from deep, safe water into the thin stuff to feed, until you consider a couple of factors. When fish are feeding heavily, they forgo their priority for safety somewhat, at least until something interrupts them. And, in order to be efficient in their feeding, they do it in places where it's easy. It's easy where the density of food is high. A shallow spot in a stream is a constriction in the channel that projects up from the bottom, and the greatest concentration of food is here, where the current carries food through the shallows. These are areas of more food in less space.

But not just any shallow water will do. It has to both produce food and deliver it to the fish. There should be a gravel bottom where lots of aquatic insects live, and medium to quick current to provide oxygen and present the nymphs conveniently to the fish. Maybe you've noticed that such a

they land with a splat that spooks trout in shallow water. I prefer either the plastic sleeve indicator that slides over the leader and lodges on a knot (these are short pieces of fly line with the core removed), or a small piece of brightly-coloured yarn. The yarn can be attached to the leader several ways. A piece can be inserted into the loop of either a Double Surgeon's Knot or a simple slip knot before the knot is pulled tight. Another way is to tie a piece of mono parallel to the tippet using a Duncan Loop Knot and insert the yarn into the loop before tightening. The latter method creates a moveable indicator. Once the yarn is attached, trim the ends short and treat it with floatant. For this kind of fishing the indicator is simply a marker so use the smallest one you can see. Depending on the depth and speed of the water, it should be positioned on the leader one to three feet from the fly.

Fly selection is important in this type of fishing, but not so much for the pattern as for the size and weight. The nymph must be heavy enough to break the surface and sink immediately, but small enough that it doesn't make a fish-spooking commotion when it hits the water. I often use a weighted Hare's Ear or Pheasant Tail nymph in size 14 or 16. A wire-bodied fly like the South Platte Brassie is also good because it makes no disturbance when it hits the water, yet sinks immediately, even if it's very small. If the fly doesn't sink to the fish's depth quickly enough, I prefer to switch to a slightly heavier nymph rather than add weight to the leader.

Shallow water nymphing is almost always an upstream game. You work your way along methodically, making each cast farther upstream than the last. Wade carefully and quietly and presume you're stalking a wild animal, because you are. Your casts should be short, in the 20 to 30-foot range. Watch the indicator carefully and strike quickly but gently when it hesitates. Remind yourself that you need a "5X hook-set," and not a "1X yank."

It's worth learning to make a tuck cast, which is simply a downward curve cast that sends a weighted nymph straight down into the water. The fly lands before the leader and line do, which gives the fly a head start on sinking before it's affected by the pull of the current on the leader and line.

A tuck cast gets the fly slightly deeper than a conventional cast, and by using it selectively you can vary the depth at which you fish without having to add weight or change flies as often.

Under certain conditions shallow-water nymphing becomes sight nymphing, which ranks only slightly below casting to rising fish on many fly fishers' entertainment scales.

It is best done on a sunny day when the water is clear and you have an elevated streambank from which to spot fish. It's easiest with two people – one spotting and one casting. The spotter functions as a coach/consultant/advisor who watches the fish, directs the casts, suggests fly changes and tells the caster if the fish changes position, eats the fly, or flees the scene in fear.

If you really want to have fun, do this without an indicator. The spotter must then interpret the fish's behaviour to determine when the fly has been eaten. With a perfect cast, the nymph drifts a few inches to the near side of the fish, rather than right at the fish. When the fly comes right to the fish, it's hard to recognize a take because the fish doesn't have to move to get the fly. A fly that passes three inches to one side of the fish requires a slight move in that direction by the fish, and that movement is the spotter's cue to yell "strike" as loud as he can to try and startle his partner into snapping the fish off. If, as the spotter, you are successful at this manoeuvre, remember: your turn is coming.

One of the reasons we fish with flies is because it allows us to participate in the trout's world. And the more I fish, the more I am drawn to the shallow water where even the big fish sometimes feed, and where the boundary that separates their world from ours, though absolute, is only a few inches wide.

CHAPTER 9

2006

Though it's sometimes hard to accept, a fly fisher's calendar consists of two parts: the part for fishing, and the part for things other than fishing. The latter is what we call the off-season, and I've decided there are some benefits to having one. They include, of course, the opportunity to restock brownie points with spouses, bosses, and other influential parties, but there's also the benefit that comes from reflecting on what occurred during the past fishing season. By doing so, if we're wise and perceptive, we may realize an increase in our understanding of fish, fishing, and ourselves.

The past fishing season has already begun its descent into the murky channels of my memory where it will soon become assimilated with and absorbed by the other 40 or so fishing seasons that rattle around there in the dark. Before too much time goes by I should try to figure out what I learned.

Lesson I: The Resilience of Rivers

In 2005 some of the worst flooding in over a hundred years occurred on many of the best trout streams in west central and southwestern Alberta. This caused great concern among fly fishers about how much the flood would damage streams, the trout, and the things the trout eat. Yet the majority of streams slammed by the floods fished very well in 2006, and many produced substantially bigger fish than usual. So the first lesson from 2006 was simply the reinforcement of something I'm already supposed to know – that trout and trout streams are resilient things, more than capable of withstanding the forces of Mother Nature. It's Man and his long list of big ideas that causes most of their trouble.

Lesson II: The Semi-Reliable Hatch

One thing rivers and trout teach us all the time is to stop thinking we know so much. I've often said that the most reliable time to find rising trout on western streams is on cloudy or showery September afternoons, because those conditions consistently bring strong hatches of *Baetis* or Blue-winged Olive mayflies. I'm changing my tune after 2006, and striking the words *reliable* and *consistently* from my discourse. The reason is that on at least three occasions in the fall of 2006 I managed to be on good water under the prescribed conditions, and each time somebody forgot to tell the bugs about the plan. I'm still waiting for the first Blue-winged Olive.

Lesson III: Give Me a Dumb Fish – Please!

On the other hand, sometimes the trout follow through and do exactly what's expected. Unfortunately, this seems to happen most often when it involves avoiding fishermen. One summer evening a friend and I found ourselves on a slow, flat pool on the Crowsnest River in southwestern Alberta. The weather was bright, which usually reduces insect activity and numbers of rising trout, but shade comes early to this part of the river and when we arrived around 5:30 there was a nice hatch in progress and good-sized trout rising steadily and confidently. I looked at the water to see what the fish were so enthused about. The flies appeared to be *Pseudocloeon* mayflies (or whatever the taxonomists now call them). Pseudos, my friends, are nasty bugs. They're tiny – about #24, slender-bodied, and nearly transparent except for a hint of pale olive colour. Even if you can see your imitation well enough to thread a tippet through the pore-sized eye of the hook, it's a sure bet you won't be able to find it once it's on the water. I'm noticing this problem cropping up a little more often lately so I used my now standard trick of attaching a tiny speck of fluorescent yarn to the tippet about a foot from the fly. When I can't see the fly, I can almost always see the yarn, so I have a pretty good idea where the fly has to be.

My friend and I agree that our favourite kind of fishing is casting to rising fish in challenging circumstances, and I think if pushed we'd both say that we think we're pretty good at it. Well, this was indeed challenging. We did all the things you're supposed to do with difficult fish. We used finer and finer tippets - down to 7X fluorocarbon. We used smaller and smaller flies - down to #22 Comparaduns. We fished down-and-across to the fish so they would see the fly before they saw the leader. I watched my companion make one perfect cast after another, each rewarded only by a moment of silence while his fly drifted untouched through the inspection zone. Can a trout giggle? The short summary of the story is that in two hours of casting to constantly rising fish we each had two takes.

Later, when recounting this evening to some other people, my friend put it nicely into perspective: "Here were two guys with approximately 70 years of fly-fishing experience between them, using equipment worth approximately $10,000, being outsmarted by creatures with brains approximately the size of a corn kernel." So what's the lesson here? I'm not sure, except the realization that when the playing field is tilted too far in the fish's direction, all you can do is keep hitting them with your best shot and hope one of them eventually makes a mistake.

Lesson IV: Avoid All Creeps

A couple of busy seasons of teaching fly fishing have reinforced my belief that the physical skill of fly fishing is casting. I know you don't have to be a great caster to catch trout, and I know there are some very competent

anglers out there who are only mediocre casters. They're the ones who seem almost proud of their casting shortcomings and often say things like, "I'm not a great caster, but I know I can catch fish." I can't help but be puzzled by this. It's like a golfer who can drive but can't putt. What would happen to his game if he improved his putting? What would happen to the competent angler if he improved his casting?

Among experienced fly fishers the most common problem is throwing a tailing loop on the forward cast. A tailing loop occurs when the line that's moving forward drops below the line that's extending off the rod tip. The two pieces of line cross one another and the results are tangled leaders, lost flies, and blue air in the vicinity of the caster. There are a number of causes, including applying the power too suddenly, applying the power too early, and tracing a concave path with the rod tip. But very often the root of the problem lies with what I call the "Creep and Jab." The pause after the backcast is supposed to be exactly that – a pause, which is a period of time when the rod and hand remain stationary. But many casters begin moving the rod forward slowly as soon as they've made the backcast. Then when it's time to really begin the forward cast (a moment later, after the fly line has straightened out behind) the hand is too far forward. The creeping motion has used up some of the space required for the forward cast, but to no

benefit. The caster subconsciously realizes he doesn't have enough reach left to make a proper forward cast and compensates by jabbing the rod forward, thereby creating a tailing loop. If you have tailing loop problems, videotape your casting sometime and watch for the sneaky and dastardly Creep and Jab. If you see it, discipline yourself to make the pause after the backcast a true pause and not a slow creep.

Lesson V: Who's the Boss?

On Mother's Day, my wife Lynda and I decided to combine a picnic on the river with a bit of fishing. We were hoping to find some spring caddis hatching and maybe a few fish eating them. I tried hard to be a hero by preparing a nice lunch, including dessert and a bottle of wine, and carrying it in a little cooler as we walked into a favourite stretch of water.

We were having a pleasant time sitting, eating, and watching a mother killdeer do her broken wing dance when one of us saw a fish rise. We both perked up and a few minutes later we saw another rise. "Aha," I thought." The caddis have started." Wrong. What had started was not a caddis hatch, but instead a strong hatch of good-sized midges (at least in midge terms they were good-sized – about #18). In more than 30 years fishing this river I've cast to trout rising to midges less than five times. I know the midges are there, but I've never considered them very important on this river. This day, though, they were the featured entreé item, and it wasn't long before the flat loaded up with a couple of dozen rising fish. We didn't have any midges with us because of course you don't need them on this river, but we faked it with small Parachute Adams and had one of the best dry-fly sessions of the season, each catching several big, golden-flanked brown trout.

This evening reinforced my favorite lesson from time spent in the company of trout: expect the unexpected. For no matter how much we think we know about fish and fishing, we really don't know much. The fish are in charge and we're just along for the ride.

Section Three: Bugs and Fish

"Many fly fishers can identify (or least say they can identify) any number of mayflies down to species, but when it comes to caddis-identification most of us mumble and revert to the taxonomic system favoured by my old friend and mentor, Russ Thornberry: they're either the great big brown ones or the little-bitty brown ones."

CHAPTER 1

Cold Creek Journal

1991

They say that steelheading gets in your blood, and I guess I've always wanted to find out for myself. At least as often as I hear about trips filled with enormous fish though, I hear fishermen moan about bad weather, little or no action, and rivers turning chocolate brown overnight.

Consequently, I had been both anxious and reluctant to try steelheading, but I knew I wanted to do it with experienced people when the time came. In 1988 a fishing partner invited me to accompany him on his annual fall trip to British Columbia.

Day 1, September 17

It's supposed to take perseverance and hundreds of hours, but I caught my first steelhead 20 minutes and 20 casts into the first day in spite of myself, and I'm hoping it won't be a bad omen.

Jim Butler met us in the motel coffee shop at 6:15 this morning. This is the ninth year he and Charles have fished steelhead together. He used to guide on the river, but now he fishes for fun and for these few days each fall with Charles. He delivered the message we were desperate to hear—the river is in good shape.

We drove to the put-in spot and unloaded the boat in the dark. As we headed upstream through thick fog, I realized that I wouldn't see the river until I was ready to wade in and start casting. It felt strange preparing to fish a river I couldn't see for fish I had only read about. We pulled the boat in at the mouth of Cold Creek and built a fire.

When our bones had thawed and the sky had lightened, Charles led me into the water. He had me cast a dry Muddler across and slightly downstream, then make a couple of big mends and follow the skating fly around with the rod tip until it completed its swim. I hadn't made enough casts to get the kinks out of the fly line when there was a rolling boil at the fly. "Should I do something?" I asked. Charles thought I said, "Was that something?" and replied, "Yes," so I slammed the rod tip back into foggy nothingness. "Don't do that!" he groaned.

I felt awful for both of us. At Charles' suggestion, I reeled up without even making another cast. For a minute I thought he was going to ask me to sit this one out while he caught the fish, and I'd have gladly done it. But we rested the fish and changed flies, switching to a Greased Liner, and Charles very calmly said I should try to wait until I felt the fish before striking. He said some other things too, but I didn't hear them, for I was thinking about what I had heard about steelheading; how just having a strike made a successful day, even for an experienced fisherman, and how you just don't get too many chances.

I gradually worked line back out, adding a couple of feet to each cast. When I duplicated the cast that had drawn the first strike, it happened again – that slow rolling boil. I yanked again, this time with no excuse other than habit, but with the same result. Once more I immediately reeled in. Now I was convinced the river gods would cut me off. Heavy rains would probably start in a few minutes and put the river out of shape for the rest of the trip, and I would be left with only the ugly memory of these two botched chances.

I hadn't wanted it to happen that fast. I'd wanted a little time to get a feel for the river – for the wading and the casting, and to have a chance to ask what to do when a fish comes to the fly. I hoped to have some idea of what I was trying to do before I did it, but it wasn't working out that way.

We switched to a smaller Greased Liner, and I went through the procedure again, sure now that the fish was long gone. When my cast was right, though, the fish swirled again, this time hooking itself, no doubt in an effort to simply put an end to our silly game. Before my eyes could move from the river to the reel, backing was disappearing into the fog, and I headed for dry ground to fight the fish.

It was a female, about 12 pounds, so Jim and Charles said. It looked about twice the size of the biggest trout I've ever caught, so I guess they were right. And it was perfect. Hard, silver, and strong in my hands, with not a flaw. I released the fish with Jim and Charles watching, and we put the fire out and moved downstream.

The mist lifted from the river, but I remained in a sweet fog of my own for the rest of the day. I caught two more fish while Charles landed three, and all is well in my new world.

Day 2, September 18

Rain fell overnight, and the forecast is for more. The river was clear, but we fished with the thought that today might be our last if the rain kept up or if it was heavier in the high country. This is a haunting companion to steelheading that I can't get used to—the feeling that at any moment it might be all over. All anticipation must be tempered with the reality of what the weather can do. It seems to make you grasp what has already happened more tightly than what you hope might come. "We'll get 'em tomorrow" is not an altogether comforting thought. So we fished a little more determinedly and with a little less talk.

We again went straight to the mouth of Cold Creek and built a fire. It was my turn to fish the upper half of the run, which is apparently more suited to a sinking-tip line and a wet fly. The casting and mending procedure is much the same as with the dry fly – a down-and-across swing – but Jim told me that the strike would be gentle, like a leaf touching the fly as it drifted. This time I asked what to do before I cast.

"Don't do anything," Butler said. "You have to wait until he has the fly in his mouth. When he does you'll feel a soft, mushy pull. Then you can strike."

A half-hour later a leaf brushed against my sunken fly and then turned soft and mushy and I struck. Again, backing was out the tip of the rod before I could blink. This fish didn't jump, but ran and shook its head violently. It was like being hooked to a steer. Steelhead that jump are dramatic and showy, but the ones that don't jump create their own drama through suspense, because you don't know what you're dealing with until you see the fish in the shallows near your feet. So far, every fish I've caught has given me the shakes.

What continues to plague me is my inability to read the water. Jim says that steelhead want boulders on the bottom in combination with water the right depth and speed. The boulders and depth I can find, but the speed has me baffled. To my eyes the river flows very uniformly and the changes Butler sees are not apparent to me. Several times today he pointed and said, "See where the water slows down over there?" Most of the time I said yes, but the real answer was usually no. When I fished the water he pointed to though, my fly behaved differently, and it was from these places that the steelhead would invariably come.

After dinner tonight we tied a couple of flies and started a log on the motel stationery. It tells quite a story. After just two days, the three of us have landed 14 steelhead. But as always and especially after an all-day drizzle, our minds are on the weather.

Day 3, September 19

It was clear and cold this morning and the river actually dropped slightly overnight. We were elated. We fished in heavy fog at Cold Creek again this morning, and Charles caught a 14-pound hen. This is Butler's favourite piece of water. I'm beginning to see why.

The best part of this whole business is being able to catch the fish on dry flies. Sometimes you hook them the first time they come to the fly, which is okay, but it's even better when they swirl at the fly but don't take the first time. Jim and Charles call these fish "comers."

When this happens the game becomes more like conventional dry-fly fishing, for you know the precise location of a fish that is almost certain to rise again. The difference is you can be almost as sure that the fish will weigh between 10 and 20 pounds. I've caught my share of fish, and am generally pretty cool, but when I know there's a 30-incher waiting for my dry fly, I find it very hard to stay calm.

After you've located a comer, you usually rest the fish and change flies. It takes about five minutes with shaking hands. Then you cast again, knowing exactly where the strike will come from. As the fly swims its way lazily into the danger zone, the anticipation is almost unbearable. You know what's going to happen and you talk to yourself: "Don't screw it up. Don't do anything, *anything*, until you feel the weight of the fish on the line." Then it happens – the swirling boil, bringing the question that seems to require an eternity to be answered: "Is he there? No? Yes? No?" No. Reel in, rest the fish, change flies, and take a few deep breaths.

Try it again. The fly wobbles toward the place, and everything disappears from your mind but a tiny spot that is the "V" of the waking fly. The fish swirls again, this time showing a rosy side, but he's still not there. The fly swims through six more feet of ominous quiet, then another boil, more violent this time, and you feel the steady pull of something on the other end. Now you strike, the fish explodes, and your mind tries to keep up. You holler.

I enjoy the fight, but it's these extended episodes with individual fish that make the game genuinely intoxicating. Charles caught a fish today that came to four different flies before taking the fifth. He had another rise eight times before it lost interest and quit the game.

Jim Butler uses this to his advantage, I've discovered. Twice today he interrupted my casting to call me upstream to fish a specific piece of water. Both times I caught steelhead. He denies it, but I'm pretty sure he fishes till he has one come to his fly and then intentionally pulls it away from the fish. Then he calls one of us over, knowing the fish will probably rise again.

Day 4, September 20

We had a tough day today – the kind you're told to expect in steelheading. Today the stories of hours of unproductive casting came true. I had two strikes and landed one fish – a three pounder – and Charles had one strike.

I'd been anticipating one of these days, wondering how I would react. It's funny, but it's not that bad. One reason is that it can all change with the next cast, and if you think about it, the difference between good

steelheading and poor is not really that much.

You don't need many of these fish. One steelhead will go a long ways, both literally and figuratively, and if they were too plentiful or too easy, much of the novelty and specialness would disappear. Gems are treasured because they're rare not because they're common.

Each morning at six we go to our regular booth in the coffee shop and Jim arrives for one cup. Then Charles fidgets while I eat too much breakfast. The drive to the put-in spot, the unloading of the boat, the trip up river to Cold Creek, the fire, and alternating the upper and lower halves of the run are the same each day, but I'm finding the routine comforting rather than tedious.

Day 5, September 21

Steelheading is like baseball, where managers look at long-term tendencies and develop a strategy based on past performance. Something that's successful today isn't really notable until it has proven itself over the long term. When the guide says that in the past this run has produced fish at this time of year with this fly and this method, you fish that way. If it doesn't work today or tomorrow, you don't give up on it, for it might work the next day.

There are a lot of questions in steelheading. There are plenty of answers, too, but few of them will ever be confirmed. A rather rudimentary one is "why does the steelhead take the fly?" Most experts agree that the fish are not feeding when they're in these rivers, so another reason must be found. The aggression theory says that the fish view the fly as an intruder and are stirred to attack it. A cynic would ask why they don't take it more violently if it is an act of aggression.

More specifically, why does a huge, non-feeding fish come to the surface for a skating dry fly? This seems to be the biggest question, and one theory to explain it is called juvenile retention. The fish are thought to carry a subconscious memory of their habit of feeding on skittering stoneflies and caddisflies during their first year of life. This memory is supposedly triggered by the sight of a skating dry fly. But somebody didn't think of this theory and then use it to catch the fish. Instead, it happened the other way around. Somebody – probably an Atlantic salmon fisherman – tried it and found that steelhead will take a dry fly, and then a retroactive theory was needed to explain it.

There's nothing wrong with trying to figure all this out; that's human nature. Likewise, there is nothing wrong with not knowing the answers. It's a marvelous mystery that these fish do what they do, and I'm content to leave it at that.

Day 6, September 22

Tonight Charles wrote on the motel stationery, "Cool, cloudy – a steelhead day." It was.

For the sixth consecutive day we started the morning at Cold Creek, and for the sixth consecutive day we hooked a fish there. Near the bottom of the run, I thought I saw a wake under my fly as it neared the end of a swing. I made another cast, and a fish boiled but didn't take. The fly was now sunk, but I let it continue its swing. As the line straightened out, there was the most violent strike I've had. It was a hen and my biggest so far.

The steelhead we are catching are 200 miles from the ocean on their way upriver to spawn next spring. Jim told me about a fish that biologists caught and fitted with a radio transmitter to track its migration. It came up through the Skeena system and entered the Kispiox River, then apparently decided it was in the wrong neighborhood. It went back to the ocean, 300 miles south along the coast, and up the into the Fraser system.

Every time he watches you release a fish, Jim Butler pronounces a sort of benediction: "Go and make babies." I feel a little humbled by the magnitude of the fish's migration, and a little embarrassed for interrupting their journey for such a trivial thing as my recreation. With all his experience, though, Butler seems to carry the same emotions and I take comfort in that.

I guess everybody doesn't feel these things, though, for there are still plenty of steelhead in fishermen's freezers. I'm being condescending now, but nonetheless, knowing where these fish have been and where they're going, I can't imagine killing one. They are one of nature's most perfect creatures and have far more claim to these rivers than we do.

Day 7, September 23

I feel sorry for many of my friends who've gone steelheading for the first time on their own. Not only is steelheading very different from trout fishing, but all steelhead rivers are different from each other. If I had been on my own for these seven days, even with a boat and the right flies and detailed descriptions of where and how to fish, I would have been lucky to hook a couple of steelhead. By far the most important part of steelheading is not tackle or flies, but knowledge of the river.

In that regard, Butler's final performance was a classic. This afternoon he had me start at the top of a long run and work down. At a point two-thirds of the way through, he waded out and said, "Okay, you're getting to the good water now, but you're wading a little too deep. Take about three steps back before you cast again."

If I've learned anything on this trip, it's to do what these guys tell me. I took my three steps back, made my cast and caught my steelhead. Just like that. One cast. I asked him how he knew and with a grin he pointed and said, "See where the water slows down out there..."

As the trip comes to a close, I'm left with a lot of feelings. Among them is a sense that I've cheated the odds. I've caught more steelhead in my first week that many people do in several years, and I almost feel guilty for not having properly paid my dues.

I'm also left with a lot of memories – of the first fish, the last fish, and the brute strength of all the fish. As with most fly fishing, though, there's more to it than that, and I know I will long ponder the miracle of the steelhead's migration and the marvelous way they come to the fly.

CHAPTER 2

The San Juan Worm

1988

We fly fishers have really painted ourselves into a corner this time. This new fly on the scene is causing quite a stir. It looks like a worm. That's right, a worm. We all know real fly fishermen don't use bait, so they certainly wouldn't be interested in using a fly that looks like a worm, would they? End of discussion, right? Not quite. There's one problem. The thing really catches fish – sometimes more fish than all the old standbys put together.

So what's a guy supposed to do? If he uses it, some will say he has fallen from grace and can no longer be called a true fly fisherman. On the other hand, if he remains pure, he just might be missing out on a pretty good thing. There were several positions taken when this issue arose in my neck of the woods a few years ago.

Some fishermen used the fly immediately, guilt or no guilt. Others steadfastly refused on moral grounds. The most fun to watch, though, were those who changed their stance through the course of the fishing season. Initially, before they knew how well this fly worked, many fishermen ranted and raved, saying it was unethical to use it, and anybody who did wasn't really fly fishing. By late July however, there was some serious back-pedaling going on.

"Well," a local guide told me, "I let my clients fish with it but I certainly wouldn't use one myself." A little later when somebody caught him with one tied to his own leader he said, "I thought I better figure out the best way to fish these things—you know, so I can be of more help to my clients." The next time I checked in, he not only admitted using the worm, but he also described in glowing terms the details of his own new version of the fly, which he had by then named after himself.

The fly in its most common form was popularized on the San Juan River in New Mexico, although its origins are somewhat hazy. I was told by a fisherman from that state that it started out in small sizes - 14 and 16 – as a red midge larva imitation. Fishermen began to experiment with larger and larger versions and found that the big ones seemed to work better. At some point in this growth the fly began to imitate a different organism, for in the San Juan River there live large numbers of thin, aquatic worms that look very much like earthworms. They apparently are true aquatic worms of the family *Lumbriculidae*. In another version of the story, Gary Borger, in *Naturals*, describes a different San Juan Worm – one that was initially supposed to imitate a scud, but also represented the worms very well.

Fishermen who used the fly with success in New Mexico found that it worked well other places too, for it turns out these aquatic worms live in the sand and silt of many trout rivers. The fly was very popular on Montana's Bighorn in 1985 and I first heard of it being used on Alberta's Bow River in 1986. Since then it has become a standard on many big western rivers and spring creeks. The fly is now used in a wide range of sizes, but seems most popular in 8 through 12.

In each of the rivers where it has become popular, the San Juan Worm made a big splash, if you'll pardon the expression, when first introduced to the stream. It truly is remarkable the way fish responded to it. Guides on the Bighorn told me fussy brown trout would often move six feet out of their way to take "the worm." On the Bow it was relatively popular in 1986, but in 1987 it was far and away the most consistent producer. A friend of mine reported that the worm turned a very mediocre day into a spectacular one on Montana's Missouri River in September of 1987. His guide had heard of, but not used the fly, and was astounded at its effectiveness. It also quickly caught on in the Yellowstone and Crowsnest rivers.

What's interesting is, in the case of the San Juan and Bighorn rivers, after a couple of years of great productivity the fly's effectiveness decreased to the point where it is now just another good fly. It will be interesting to see if that happens on the other rivers.

If you had to put it into one of the conventional classes of trout flies, I guess you'd call it a nymph – not because it imitates the larval form of anything, but because of the way it is fished. The standard procedure is to drift it along the bottom in the same choppy water where you might fish a stonefly nymph or caddisfly larva. Though it works in slow water, like most true nymphs it is easier to fish in faster, more broken sections of stream. Most people like to fish it upstream, casting above the expected lie of the fish and letting the fly dead-drift through the hot spot. The most consistently successful anglers add large doses of lead to the leader to get the fly deep. The faster and/or deeper the water, the more lead required. You have to leave your prejudices against lead-lobbing at home.

There are new variations of the San Juan Worm being created all the time. In 1987, Bow River fishermen experimented with different colours, including fluorescent red and yellow, and some used them as large as size 2. Some used red ostrich herl for the bodies, and some used Swanundaze. They all work.

The one unanswered question is why this fly works so well. I don't think anyone knows for sure, but I can venture a couple of guesses. First, it represents an organism the fish see and feed on regularly. This alone would make it work. I think what makes it work so well is the fact that it represents a natural food very few anglers have tried to imitate in the past. It may be that these aquatic worms have been the one thing trout have always been able to eat without the threat of being stung by a hook. This may also explain why the fly's effectiveness has tapered off in some rivers. The fish have learned to be as skeptical about aquatic worm imitations as they are about standard dry flies, streamers, and nymphs.

I also believe it works well because it is a thin, streamlined fly that sinks very quickly. Experiments in my early days of nymphing convinced me that the fatter and fuzzier a nymph is, the slower it sinks due to water resistance on the body of the fly and all the little fibres sticking out. The worm is thin and has no fuzz, so it really gets down quickly.

So, the question remains. Do real fly fishermen use San Juan Worms? I see no difference between using this fly and using an imitation of a stonefly nymph or leech. In each case, we put a hook in our tying vise (if we tie our own flies) and attach stuff to the hook in a way we hope will represent a particular natural organism the fish see and feed on regularly. Then we tie it to our leader and try to fish it in a manner consistent with the behaviour of the natural. This all falls comfortably within my personal definition of fly fishing. (The real problem with this fly is its name. We'd all feel better if it was the San Juan Nymph, or the San Juan Creeper or almost anything else. "Worm" is probably the most offensive word in the English language to staunch fly fishermen.)

The question then, must be answered by each individual. It doesn't bother me to use the fly, but others may not agree. I was chastised once for encouraging people to take up nymph fishing. The argument was that I was contributing to the "cleaning out" of our streams. My response to that seems to fit here, too. What one attaches to the hook that catches the fish is a matter of concern only to the angler. While fish caught on live bait cannot usually be released safely, the fish don't really care whether the angler casts spinning lures, jigs, wet flies, or small, barbless dry flies. In the long run it matters not what a fish is caught with, but rather what happens to him once he is caught, and in each case the decision to kill or release must be considered with seriousness by the angler. And, as little Edith-Ann would say, "that's the truth."

Project Fish

1998

Have you ever gone to a lot of trouble to catch a fish? Of course you have; we all have. That's not what I mean. I mean, have you ever gone to a lot of trouble to catch one particular fish? Have you ever passed up a sure bet somewhere to try again for a fish that seems to have your number? By my definition, when you try for the same fish in the same place more than once without catching him, you've got yourself a bona fide project fish. It's not uncommon to have both dreams and nightmares about such a fish, and before you know it, the whole game can become an obsession.

For a fish to qualify, it must be found in the same spot regularly and it must at least give the impression of being catchable. Migratory fish like salmon and steelhead don't count, and neither do bass, pike, or saltwater fish. Project fish are almost always trout, usually trout in small streams, and most often browns. The reason is that brown trout in small streams are homebodies that stay in their lies until somebody or something moves them out.

I've had many project fish over the years, some of which I've caught and many of which I haven't. Some - more than I'd like to admit - have become whole-season or longer propositions. The first one I remember lived in a small stream in west-central Alberta. It was a big trout for this creek, though not a monster. A friend told me about the fish, and it got under my skin a bit when he showed me a picture. He had caught and released the fish a couple of times, which made it even more important for me to catch the trout and take my own photograph of it. In this case I finally did, on about my fifth attempt, and in doing so felt I had gained admission into a kind of elite and secret club. Somewhere in my office I still have a wrinkly old print of this fish we called "the tree hole trout."

A few years later another friend called one night to tell me he'd caught Walter. "Walter?" I said. "Yeah, you know, the big brown that lives under the bank upstream of the ford on Frenchman's Creek. I've been trying to catch him for two years." Oh, that Walter.

Another big brown trout in another stream became my obsession after I found him rising on three consecutive trips but couldn't fool him. On my next visit he took a #14 Adams on the first cast. It was an enormous fish, and I was feeling pretty smug right up until my new braided leader came apart. The trout swam slowly off downstream with a fly and half a leader. I looked for this fish many times afterwards but never saw him again.

Some fish seem to be aware of the game, and not catching them simply becomes part of your duty when you visit that stream. There is a fish in another creek that seems to be rising every time I'm there. I've tried for him at least a dozen times and have never had him give even a cursory look at my fly. When I mentioned this fish to my friend who owns the land along the creek, he said "Oh, that guy. He rises all the time, but nobody's ever caught him." I don't know about you, but that's exactly the kind of taunt I fall for. It would be pretty cool to catch the uncatchable fish, wouldn't it? If I caught him, I'd get to name him. That's the way it works, doesn't it? But I know I probably won't catch the uncatchable trout, and that's okay. These fish are a kind of never-ending project, the type I've come to think we need in fly fishing, if for no other purpose than to preserve humility.

There is great satisfaction in finally winning one of these encounters, but the bittersweet trade off is in the fact that the long quest ends when you catch the fish. Most of the magic disappears when you put him in your net.

The Bead Goes On

1994

Picture this. Five different tribes of primitive people in different parts of the world are each given a violin. It comes with no instructions and no indication of its purpose. Each tribe is told only that it is useful and must be integrated into their culture. Two hundred years later there would likely be a number of drastically different uses made of the fiddle. Some tribes might actually use it to make music, but others might have discovered that it's a terrific agricultural tool or maybe a weapon.

There are some similarities between the violin story and the way our sport of fly fishing has developed. I realized this in the spring of 1993 when I was in Kamloops while the World Fly Fishing Championships were taking place there. For the first time I became aware of the tremendous breadth of fly fishing's popularity. It is not simply a sport invented by the English and adopted by the Americans. It has been developing in significant ways in other parts of the world as well, and in Kamloops there were teams from Spain, Poland, Italy and dozens of other countries.

It should come as no surprise then to see that fly fishers, like our fictional fiddle players, have taken the sport in somewhat different directions over the years. Until recently, our North American superiority complex has prevented us from appreciating what other countries' fishermen have learned, but I think that's beginning to change. The Kamloops trip and other exposure to European fly fishers have convinced me that North Americans don't have a monopoly on good ideas.

A couple of years ago the soft, "butt of the duck" feathers, called *cul de canard* or CDC, migrated from Europe where they have been an important fly-tying material for years, and last year it was bead-head flies. The bead-head idea developed in Italy and Germany and was shown to North American fly tiers by the German fly-fishing guru, Roman Moser.

After I experimented with bead-heads in 1992, my fly shop decided to stock a couple of patterns in 1993. At first they didn't sell very well, and when most fishermen saw them they responded with predictable North American skepticism: "What's *that*?" We simply told people to try them and let us know how they worked. It wasn't long before the bead-head bins were empty and from then on it was difficult to keep enough in the shop.

The beads are usually brass, copper, silver, or black, and slide over the point of the hook and around to rest against the eye. Because the bead is solid, it adds more weight to the fly than a conventional underwrap of wire. The result is a small fly that sinks very quickly. They get down to where the fish live, thereby accomplishing the number one objective in nymph fishing, which is to make it easy for the fish to take the fly.

The bead also gives the fly a point of sparkle at the front that probably attracts the fish's attention, even from some distance. During emergence many insects, particularly caddisfly pupae, develop an air bubble inside their skin that catches and reflects light much the way a small bead does.

Another theory says that the bead causes the fly to ride differently in the water than a conventional nymph. A standard nymph probably rides with the head up and tail down, but a bead-head may ride head down or at least more level because of the concentration of weight at the front, and perhaps this is more appealing to the fish.

At any rate, a bead-head is a small fly that sinks quickly, attracts fish's attention, and has a wink of sparkle that suggests life to the trout. Pretty simple, right? Okay then, why didn't we think of it?

CHAPTER 5

Fly Fishing for Western Pike

2004

This story is not for the squeamish. A man was fly fishing for pike on a western irrigation reservoir one quiet spring morning. Blackbirds were singing from cattails around the marshy edges of the lake and waterfowl were cutting the sky. He was casting around the neck of a small bay when a hen mallard and a string of seven fuzzy yellow ducklings came paddling out of the bay towards him. The serenity was crushed by a violent implosion of water punctuated by quacking and flapping. Duck and ducklings scattered like water drops on a hot stove. When the spray settled, duckling number seven was gone. We've all heard a version of this story that ends here, but in this case the angler was a practical sort and immediately pitched his fly toward the place where the crime was committed. He made a couple of strips on his fly line and had a vicious take from a good-sized pike. He played and landed the fish, wondering if it was the same one that had just eaten the duckling. While unhooking the fish he saw a bulge in the fish's stomach and put his hand there. He could feel something inside, and it was moving.

This is one of those stories that can't be traced to the source, so it may or may not be true. But the fact that it could be true says plenty about the character and attitude of the northern pike. And a story about pike would not be complete until the author pointed out knowingly that the Latin name for the fish, *Esox lucius*, means "water wolf." There, done.

This water wolf has a huge natural range, extending through Europe, Asia, and North America. On our continent they can be found from Alaska to Missouri, and from British Columbia to Labrador.

They are often described as warm water fish, but that title usually comes from trout fishermen who feel all species other than trout should be dumped into that second-rate category. Pike could better be called "cool water fish" since they thrive in water that ranges from barely liquid in winter to temperatures in the low 20s Celsius in summer (not much different than the trout's range). Their preferred habitat is shallow, weedy, clear water and while they're primarily a lake fish they also live in slow moving rivers if the habitat is right. They are the main attraction at many wilderness fishing lodges in the North and are common in lakes and irrigation impoundments through the prairie regions of western Canada and the western U.S.

Anglers like pike because they're one of few freshwater fish that can be measured in feet rather than inches. Hardware fishermen have known this for decades, but we fly fishers are a bit hard-headed and have only recently discovered pike fishing in a big way.

Fly rods and northern pike are a natural fit because pike are aggressive, ambush-style feeders that like shallow water. Their strikes are sudden, violent, frightening, and addictive. A friend of mine declares shamelessly that it's the gratuitous violence that attracts him to pike fishing.

Trout purists in the West are climbing on the pike bandwagon because they've learned that the best pike fishing occurs when adjacent trout streams are dirty from spring runoff. In Alberta and Montana, prime time for fly-rod pike fishing is mid-May through mid-June.

Northern pike are one of many cogs in the complex ecosystem of the western prairie. At first glance a flat, prairie lake might not be as attractive as a trout stream in the high country, but on closer inspection it's clear that there's a lot going on here. A marshy lake and the land surrounding it is not merely alive, it's downright busy. Shore birds tiptoe across mud flats, ducks gabble amongst themselves, a prairie falcon stoops on a covey of partridge flushed from a barley field. For a fly fisher, this is the place to be on a lazy June afternoon when the air thickens, the western sky blackens and the mood of the water wolf turns surly.

A Pike's Life

Pike grow to huge sizes, but it's a long process. Their growth rate varies greatly with latitude. Females can reach a length of 30 inches in five or six years in the southern part of their range, but it takes much longer in the North. The fish we're most interested in catching—the three to four-footers—are always females and usually senior citizens. It takes a long time to grow a trophy pike and that's one of the reasons stocks of large pike are depressed in some parts of the West. The big fish are simply being harvested faster than they are being produced.

Pike that make it safely through winter without falling into the clutches of an ice fisherman move into shallow water just as the ice recedes. The smaller males arrive first, then the larger females. It's a poor time for fishing, as the fish are preparing to spawn and have matters other than food on their minds. Spawning lasts a couple of weeks and takes place in shallow water where there is vegetation on the bottom and along the shoreline. After spawning the pike remain in the shallow bays as the water continues to warm. It is during this period, when the fish are recovering from spawning and are feeding actively, that fly fishing is best.

The post-spawn feeding peaks as the water temperature approaches 15 degrees Celsius. Few living creatures near the water are safe when this is going on. That rattling commotion over in the cattails is a pike running a school of small whitefish. That "something" that startles a wading angler when it brushes against his leg is a big female flushed from her hunting grounds. Even the blackbirds are nervous.

Once the water rises above the magic mark, pike move to deeper water. It's not specifically depth they are seeking, but rather water of suitable temperature. They spend the summer in deeper water and move back into shallower areas again in the fall as the water cools.

Catching Pike on Flies

Where and When

In order to catch a pike, we must first find a pike lake. It's usually not hard. Most tackle shops or sporting goods stores know where they are. The clerks may or may not know about fly fishing for pike, but they'll know where the fish are. Ask them to describe some of the lakes and then choose one that has an abundance of shallow water, plenty of bays and islands, and lots of vegetation both in the water and along the shoreline.

When to fish for pike is a function of the season, and timing varies significantly with latitude. In southern Alberta, Saskatchewan, and Montana, the post-spawn feeding binge takes place between mid-May and mid-June. It occurs later in the northern parts of the pike's range and earlier in the south. In the North, fly fishing for pike often remains good right through summer because the water never gets warm enough to drive the fish out of the shallows.

Choosing a Spot

Just finding a lake with pike in it isn't good enough. We need to pick a good spot on the lake. Look for shallow areas with reedy shorelines, small islands, underwater weed beds, and abundant food in the form of small fish. Once you find a spot, check the water temperature. If it's within two or three degrees of 15 degrees Celsius, start fishing. If it's cooler than that, look for a place where the water is warmer. This might be a shallower bay or a place where the bottom of the lake is dark-coloured and has absorbed more heat from the sun. It could also be a place where the wind blows directly into a shallow bay. This pushes the warm upper layer of water into the bay where it collects and attracts pike. In spring the north ends of prairie lakes are generally a little warmer than the south ends.

If the water is much warmer than 15 degrees, well, "you shoulda been here last week." Still, try deeper water, a bay with a light-coloured bottom, the south end of the lake, or a place where a cool tributary or spring enters.

How

Once a spot is selected it's important to have a logical plan of attack. If there is no wind, a surface fly might work. Cast it towards the shoreline or some other cover, remembering that pike prefer to ambush their prey rather than chase it down. Resist the temptation to retrieve as soon as the fly lands. Instead, let it rest on the surface until the rings disappear, and then twitch the fly so it makes a pitiful disturbance on the surface. The strikes will be sudden and violent. Try not to fall in when the fish takes, and don't do this at all if your heart (or bladder) is weak.

For unknown reasons, surface flies work most consistently in the northern part of the pike's range. Near my home in southern Alberta they are occasionally productive, but in northern Alberta and northern Saskatchewan topwater flies work well a good part of the time.

If the fish won't come to the surface for a "dry fly," the fly must be taken down to the fish. A good choice is a Deceiver or Bunny type fly. After the first cast make a quick, stripping retrieve as soon as the fly lands. After the second cast let the fly sink for a five-count before beginning the same retrieve. On the third cast let it sink for a count of ten, and so on. Then go through the same sequence with slower retrieves. If the water is deep enough, switch to a sinking-tip fly line and work the fly deeper still. Be sure to move the casts around to thoroughly cover the area. Try a couple of different coloured flies during the process. If none of this works, move to another spot.

Getting Around

The best vehicle for pike fishing is a boat - ideally a flat-bottomed johnboat powered by a reliable outboard motor. This provides great mobility and a stable platform from which to cast. It's even better if the boat is rigged with a raised casting deck because the increased elevation allows the caster to see into the water to try and locate fish visually. Float tubes and pontoon boats also work, though they have obvious disadvantages in elevation and mobility. Once a hot spot is located, it's sometimes productive to wade and fish for pike. If the water is shallow and the bottom is firm I like to wade out into the water and cast back towards the reedy shoreline.

Gear For Pike

Fly tackle for pike is not unusual, it's just bigger than what most people use for trout. Most experts favour 8- or 9-wt rods, but the power isn't for fighting the fish, but rather for delivering the fly. Pike flies are routinely three to six-inches long and as Alberta pike expert Rolf Schwabe says, "Casting a wet pike streamer with a light rod is like hitting a fastball with a broomstick."

Even though big pike rarely make long runs a large fly reel is still an asset. Pike often strike after the angler has retrieved 65 feet of a 75-foot cast. A large-arbor reel or a large conventional reel properly filled with line and backing will pick this slack line up quickly.

Most pike fishing can be done with a standard weight forward floating fly line, though a sinking-tip is useful at times. There are special pike and bass lines available with exaggerated weight-forward tapers to make it easier to deliver big flies.

The leader is the most unusual part of the pike outfit. It doesn't need be long, but it does need a 6 to12-inch "shock tippet" on the end to prevent the pike's teeth from cutting the fly off. The two most popular types of shock tippet are flexible coated wire and 30 to 60 lb monofilament. A simple pike leader can be made by tying a shock tippet to the end of a 9-foot, 0X trout leader with an Albright Knot. The fly can be attached to a wire shock tippet with a figure eight knot (2-turn clinch knot) or to a mono shock tippet with a Homer Rhodes Loop Knot. Among pike experts there are proponents of both mono and wire for shock tippets. The mono is less visible, but more prone to cutoffs from fish. Some people prefer wire, partly because it doesn't leave as many flies in fish's mouths and also because of the erratic motion imparted to the fly after the wire gets kinked.

There are some additional items that belong in a pike kit. Jaw spreaders are designed to hold a pike's mouth open while the angler removes his fly. A good adaptation is to blunt the ends of the wire on the spreaders by covering them with plastic beads. Long nosed pliers or heavy-duty forceps are necessary for fly retrieval but should first be used to pinch the barbs on the flies. It's one thing to get a size 16 trout fly stuck in your neck, and another thing altogether when it's a 2/0 pike fly. De-barbed hooks also come out of fish easier.

A hook hone is essential because the stainless steel hooks usually used for pike flies are rarely sharp as they come out of the box. Wire cutters are helpful for cutting shock tippet.

A recent development for pike fishing is the cradle net. It's a piece of mesh netting strung between two three-foot dowels. This allows large pike to be subdued and controlled with little risk of damage to the fish or fishermen. Don't be tempted to bring a big pike into the boat. Many things will be broken, perhaps some of them bones.

Speaking of damage to fishermen, be sure to carry some Band-Aids. If the fishing gets good, at some point a pike's tooth will probably contact an angler's thumb.

Flies

Pike flies are most different from trout flies in their size. They are commonly tied on hooks from size 2 through 4/0 and their overall length sometimes reaches eight inches. They are not generally intended to represent a specific food item, but rather to appeal to the pike's proclivity to kill and eat things. If the "thing" appears to be alive, or better yet in some kind of distress, Ms. Pike will probably come to the party.

Pike flies are created to meet three objectives: depth, movement and castability. Foam poppers and deer-hair flies are designed to stay on or near the surface. Lead-eyed flies like Clouser Minnows are intended for deeper water. A good pike fly appears alive in the water regardless of the speed at which it's retrieved. Unfortunately, some flies with great movement are difficult to cast. A rabbit-strip fly moves beautifully but holds water and casts like a wet sponge. Flies made with long saddle hackles or synthetic Fishair have good movement and good castability.

Colour and details of the pattern are minor factors in pike flies. Bright orange, yellow, chartreuse, and red are favoured colours, along with occasional doses of black and white.

Many pike flies are tied with monofilament or wire weed guards to deflect debris away from the point of the hook. This allows us to fish in the salad where pike often lurk in early summer.

Fly fishing for pike is often very productive. It is also often very puzzling. It is not often the slam-dunk affair that some people think it should be. The inherent limitations in fly tackle—primarily the depth at which it allows us to fish—tip the scales in favour of the pike. And that, my friends, is why we do it.

CHAPTER 6

Blue Collar Caddis

2006

Mayflies are the bug-darlings of our sport. They are beautiful, delicate, and elegantly graceful in repose and in flight. Trout eat them and fishermen write scholarly books about them. And if the mayfly is a high-profile aristocrat the caddisfly is its blue-collar cousin: plain, generic, unspectacular. But just as in human society, in the underwater world heavy responsibility falls to the middle class—in this case the responsibility of feeding the trout.

It's true that there are both mayflies and caddisflies in nearly all trout streams, but it's often the plain-jane caddis that wins the popularity contest with trout. In spite of this, caddis don't get much attention from the angling entomology crowd. Many fly fishers can identify (or least say they can identify) any number of mayflies down to species, but when it comes to caddis-identification most of us mumble and revert to the taxonomic system favoured by my old friend and mentor, Russ Thornberry: they're either the great big brown ones or the little-bitty brown ones. Perhaps the problem is that caddisflies are so nondescript. There are a great many species out there, but most of the ones you meet look pretty much the same - a generic, mottled, gray-brown colour with the only obvious differences being slight variations in size. To most of us, a caddisfly is a caddisfly is a caddisfly.

All caddisflies have a complete life cycle with four stages: egg, larva, pupa, and adult. The larva corresponds to the nymph stage of a mayfly, while the pupa is an intermediate stage between larva and adult. The larva of some caddis (*Brachycentrus* and *Dicosmoecus*, for example) build cases of sand or stream-bottom debris, and the larva of others, like *Hydropsyche* spin nets to collect food. Still others, like *Ryacophila*, do neither and are sometimes referred to as "free-living" caddis larva. Upon maturity, all larvae build and seal cases in which the transformation to pupa occurs. The pupae then swim to the surface where the final emergence as adults occurs. After mating, females lay eggs either by touching or landing on the surface of the water, or by swimming beneath the water to deposit eggs on the stream bottom and vegetation. Caddis live for up to three weeks as adults and may mate and lay eggs several times.

While there are hundreds of species of caddis in trout streams, for fly-fishing purposes it makes sense to put them into three groups.

Spring Caddis (Genus *Brachycentrus*)

In recent years a pre-runoff caddis hatch has become popular with fly fishers in many parts of the Rocky Mountain West. This early-May "Mother's Day Caddis" hatch is a major entomological event on streams like the Yellowstone, Madison, and Big Hole. In Alberta these bugs are sometimes referred to as "Victoria Day Caddis" because they appear nearer that holiday in late May. They are present in the brown trout tributaries of the Red Deer and North Saskatchewan rivers, but the best fishing I've experienced has been on the Bow below Calgary just prior to runoff, and on the mainstem Red Deer below the Dickson Dam. They seem to be absent from the Crowsnest River and other streams of the Oldman system.

Adults are about size 14, and the usual colour. An important and endearing characteristic is their propensity to hatch heavily on warm, bright afternoons, unlike their post-runoff cousins, which are generally active only at dusk.

These caddis often hatch at the same time as the spring Blue-winged

Olive *Baetis* mayflies, but in my observation the trout have strong preference for the caddis. Bow River fish are famous for their ability to unanimously ignore heavy hatches of spring BWOs. These same fish will greedily gulp an occasional caddis that appears during a blanket hatch of *Baetis*. Maybe the caddis taste better. Whatever the reason, trout like this bug, and this hatch kick-starts dry-fly season on many streams.

Summer Caddis (Genus *Rhyacophila*, *Hydropsyche*, and others)

This is the biggie—the hatch that provides classic evening dry-fly fishing on

Alberta streams from the Little Smoky to the Crowsnest. They are the usual grey/brown colour, in size 14 through 18. They scorn sunlight and appear at dusk, hatching and ovipositing well into the night. The summer caddis on the Bow below Calgary are responsible for bleary eyes and decreased morning productivity in Calgary offices from late June through mid-September. The best fishing usually takes place on warm, calm evenings, but there is great day-to-day variation in activity. One night might produce a stifling hatch, evidenced by millions of empty pupal shucks along the shore the following morning, while another seemingly identical evening

might produce just a few flies.

It's usually easy to figure out that the trout are eating caddisflies—it's a summer evening, adult caddis are flying, and you see the rise forms of trout feeding on the surface. What's not so easy is figuring out which stage of caddis the fish are eating. Trout sometimes chase pupa that are swimming to the surface to emerge, and the fish's "follow-through" breaks the surface. You see what you think is a rise, but the bug may already be in the fish's gullet when you see it. The fish also take adults that rest placidly on the surface, or adults that jitter-bug across the surface. Some species of caddis have a stage similar to the spent spinner stage of a mayfly, in which dead females float awash in the film after egg laying.

But the real fly in the ointment, if you'll pardon the expression, is the fact that female adults from the common *Hydropsyche* and *Rhyacophila* genera enter the water and swim to the bottom to lay eggs. When this chore is complete, they swim back to the surface and "re-emerge" to carry on with life. This adds two more possibilities to the list of things the fish might be eating - adults swimming to the bottom, and adults swimming back to the surface after egg-laying. (This behaviour probably explains the effectiveness of traditional English winged wet flies, which are largely overlooked by fly fishers today.) It's one of Mother Nature's cruel jokes that this activity often coincides precisely with an emergence of the same species of caddis, thereby increasing even further the confusion quotient for the poor fisherman.

Fall Caddis (*Dicosmoecus*)

One good thing about this bug is the fact that it's readily identifiable. This is our largest stream caddis, imitated nicely by a #6 or #8 cinnamon-bodied Stimulator. The flies emerge in afternoons throughout the fall and are often called October Caddis. It's hard to tell how important they are to the trout, because you rarely see these bugs in large numbers, but their sheer size makes them worthy of imitation. My experience suggests that you view the fall caddis much as you do grasshoppers in late summer. That is, don't expect heavy hatches nor steadily rising trout, but instead use an imitation as a searching dry fly whenever you see adults evident along the stream. You can also take fish on imitations of fall caddis larva and pupa. Fall caddis are common on most of Alberta's best streams, including the Bow, Crowsnest, Red Deer, and the high country cutthroat streams of the Oldman and North Saskatchewan drainages.

Fishing Caddis Larva

You can fish imitations of caddis larva anytime. Conventional nymphing with a floating fly line, 9 or 10 foot leader, and strike indicator works well. Fish the flies in broken water with a gravel or cobble bottom, and try to get dead drifts near the bottom along current seams and drop offs.

Fishing Caddis Pupa

Imitations of caddis pupa can be fished exactly like the larva, in which case they represent pupa that have just begun to drift in the current prior to ascending to the surface. This is a good method to use before, or in the early stages of a caddis emergence, such as late in the afternoon on a warm, summer day.

The down-and-across swing does a good job of mimicking the behaviour of the pupa as it ascends to the surface. The cast is made quartering downstream, and the fly is allowed to swing on a tight line through a prime holding spot or into view of a rising trout. Early in the hatch it helps to add a tiny split shot to the leader above the fly. This gets the pupa deep before it begins to swing and rise to the surface. Later in the hatch the pupa can be swung just under the surface without additional weight.

You can also fish a pupa dead-drift in the surface film. My favourite pattern for this is the late Gary LaFontaine's Emergent Sparkle Pupa. It doesn't look like much in the hand, but it must look a lot like a caddis pupa in the water, because it works very well when drifted over rising fish.

Fishing Adult Caddis

The conventional up or up-and-across method of fishing a dry fly with a drag-free drift works to imitate caddis that are resting on the surface—either live adults or spent females. But it's also frequently necessary to imitate adults that move on the surface, as they do when ovipositing. Many fly-fishing writers have noted that twitching an adult caddis is most effective if the twitch is made in an upstream direction. To achieve this, position yourself up and across from the rising fish. Make a down-and-across delivery with an upstream reach cast. As the fly drifts toward the fish, move the rod downstream at the same speed as the current to allow the fly to drift drag-free into the fish's view. When the fly reaches a point four to six feet above the fish, give the fly a slight twitch with the rod tip. That's a slight twitch, not a three-foot broad-jump. The fly should jump no more than a couple of inches in an upstream direction. This often draws violent strikes from fish that ignore repeated drag-free drifts.

If you're fishing adult imitations after dark, try a pattern that is entirely black. Most eastern slope streams flow in a generally eastward direction and a black fly is often more visible than a neutral-coloured one when it's cast upstream into the lingering glare after sunset.

Adults swimming beneath the surface during egg-laying can be imitated with a winged wet fly fished with the same down-and-across swing that is used for imitating emerging pupa.

It's often worthwhile to search the water with adult caddis patterns when fish aren't rising. This is especially true during the spring and fall caddis hatches. Another option is to fish a high floating adult pattern like an Elk Hair Caddis with pupa behind it on a dropper.

A Caddis Fishing Strategy

You can often get some idea which stage of caddis the fish are eating by carefully watching the rises. Rise forms that just bulge the surface or show a fish's back but not its head suggest that the fish are feeding on ascending pupa or on adults returning to the surface after laying eggs on the bottom. Fish that occasionally burst through the surface and into the air a couple of feet are probably chasing pupa that are ascending very quickly. Fish that rise aggressively with a quick, turning slash are probably eating adults that are moving on the surface. Fish that feed with slow, dignified, head-and-tail rises might be taking adults resting motionless on the surface. Fish that rise with nearly no disturbance at all may be eating spent females that have died after laying eggs. Don't be surprised if it seems that different fish are eating different stages at the same time, because they probably are.

If the rise forms are not consistent, here's a plan you can use. However, it comes with a warning: there are no guarantees. Sometimes it works, but just about as often, it's simply a more organized way of getting frustrated:

1. If there is no surface activity but you know it's caddis season, fish a larva dead-drifted near the bottom.
2. If there are adult caddis apparent, but no fish rising, fish a larva or pupa dead-drifted near the bottom.
3. If there are caddis apparent and fish rising try this sequence:
    a. First try an adult imitation like an Elk Hair Caddis or a CDC Caddis dead-drifted over the risers.
    b. If that doesn't work, try the same fly, but give it a slight upstream twitch just as it comes into the fish's view.
    c. If that doesn't work, try a LaFontaine Emergent Caddis Pupa dead drifted over the risers.
    d. If that doesn't work, try a soft hackle wet fly fished to the risers with a down-and-across swing from an upstream position.
    e. If that doesn't work, try a winged wet fly like a Leadwing Coachman or Dark Cahill, fished to the risers with a down-and-across swing from an upstream position.
4. If the rises are very gentle, try a spent caddis.
5. If you get this far without success, go home and get some sleep.

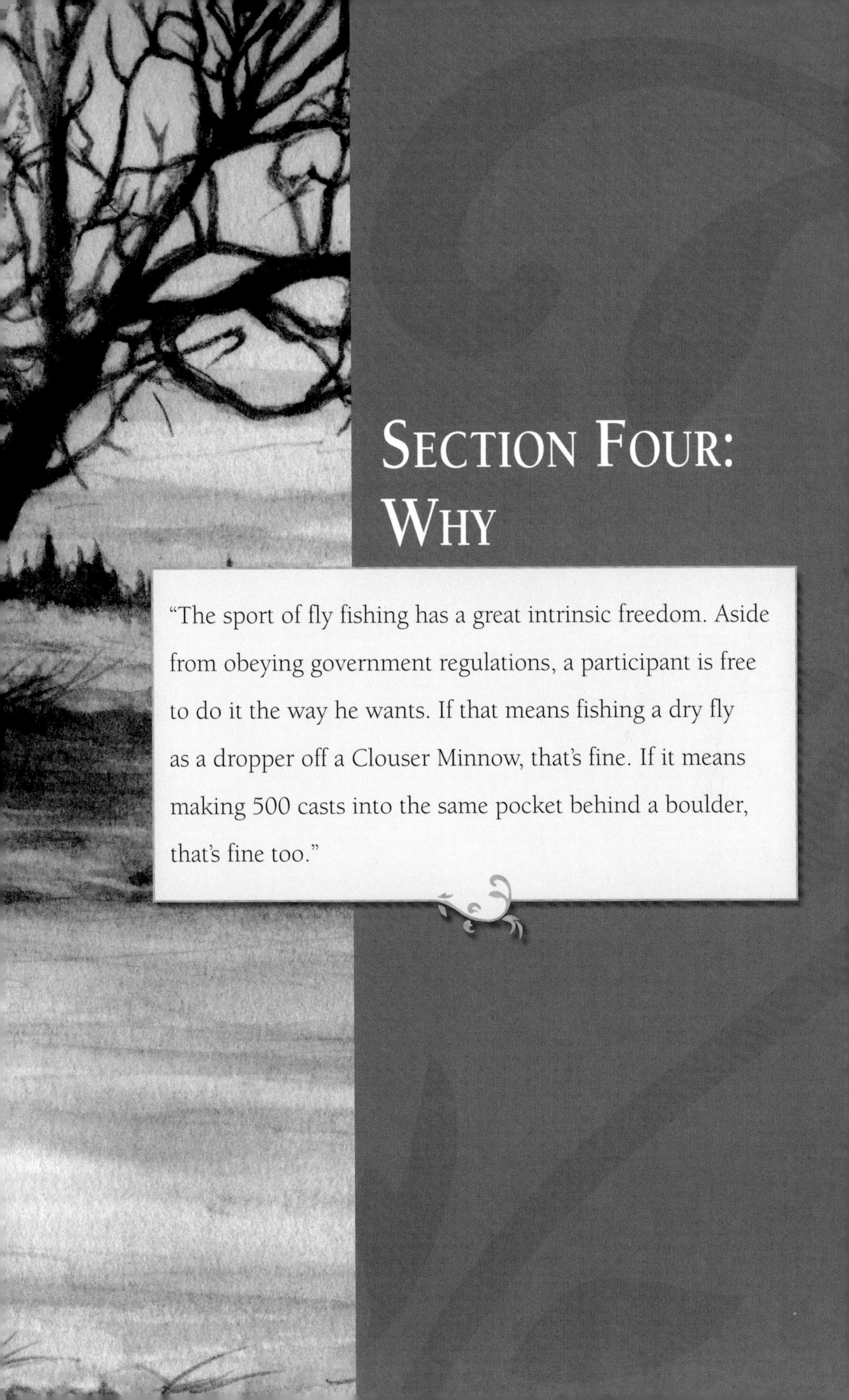

Section Four: Why

"The sport of fly fishing has a great intrinsic freedom. Aside from obeying government regulations, a participant is free to do it the way he wants. If that means fishing a dry fly as a dropper off a Clouser Minnow, that's fine. If it means making 500 casts into the same pocket behind a boulder, that's fine too."

CHAPTER 1

Bugs and Snakes

2002

The Beaverhead River was described to me once by a fishing guide as an "ugly little river." This is testament to the theory of *different strokes for different folks*. The Beaverhead is a tailwater, and a great one. There are some rainbows there, but the name of the game is brown trout.

The river flows through a wide, arid, sage-pocked valley in southwestern Montana. The only part of the valley that is green in August is a thin band of willows that densely lines the river as it winds north out of Clark Canyon Reservoir. The first time I fished the Beaverhead was on the first stop of a week-long fishing tour of Montana and Wyoming with my wife and daughter. We spent the night at the KOA campground in Dillon after soliciting fishing advice from Tim Tollett at his Frontier Anglers fly shop. The next day we drove towards the reservoir under a cloudless sky and oppressive heat, following directions Tim had scribbled on a paper napkin.

We parked in a rare, shady spot and began to shovel gear out of the van so we could rig up and fish. A few minutes into the proceedings I heard muttering from the other side of the van. My daughter Deanna, 13 at the time, had discovered that her wading shoes were still back home in Alberta. Our solution of duct-taping her street sandals onto the outside of her waders left her in an owly mood. My wife Lynda noted with equally foul demeanour that the mosquitoes seemed to really like the expensive new bug dope she was trying out.

We threw leftover gear back into the vehicle and I led the way toward the thickest willows, pretending to know where I was going, and remembering one piece of Tim's advice more strongly than the others: "Keep an eye out, there's the odd rattlesnake up there." I could hear the girls walking behind me, tripping in the tall, wet grass, muttering, swatting mosquitoes, and generally having a swell time. They hadn't heard Tim's warning about snakes, and I wasn't planning to mention it. I forged on, trying to be at least outwardly optimistic, all the while thinking to myself, "If we last 20 minutes with this heat and these bugs it will be a miracle."

When we got to the river, I tried to locate an attractive piece of water to

fish. There wasn't any. The river was high and it was difficult to do anything but fish right against the bank, but I found a small riffle where the river crowded against the railroad track. I told Lynda to fish there with the recommended Pheasant Tail Nymph while I tried to find another spot. I got myself organized downstream a short way and started to cast, wondering how much time was left on the meter, when I heard my wife yell. I looked up in time to see the better part of two feet of brown trout fall back into the water near the place where her fly line entered. The fish ran downstream a bit and then came unglued. This sudden upswing in fishing potential drew the attention of Deanna who mysteriously appeared from somewhere up-river. She elbowed her mother aside, made a few casts into the riffle, and soon made the same vocalization Lynda just had, for the same reason – and with the same ultimate end.

Mom's turn: another dozen casts and another hookup with another big brown trout. This time the trout was brought into possession with Deanna on net duty. It was perhaps the smallest of the three fish hooked, at about 20-inches long. Then out of the corner of my eye I saw a glint at the very top of the same riffle. I watched the spot and saw it again. A fish had moved up into the shallows and was picking off the Pale Morning Duns that by now were sailing by in some quantity. Deanna made a number of casts with a number of flies before the fish slid up under her Parachute PMD and sipped it. The fish turned with the current, boiled for deeper water, and was gone. Another big brown. Suddenly the mosquitoes didn't seem so bad.

As we drove on to our next destination, I got the familiar feeling that there was a lesson hiding somewhere in the day's events if I was smart enough to uncover it. I wasn't sure it had much to do with catching fish. It might have had something to do with expectations, for I couldn't help comparing this day with others when the timing, weather and water conditions seemed perfect – but the fishing turned out lousy. I'm not sure, but it could be that the message is as simple as *you never know*.

Ugly little river indeed.

CHAPTER 2

The End of the Innocence

1995

This will probably make me sound like an old fud, but there's something I need to get off my chest. It's simply this: I think we're losing touch with the essence of fly fishing, and I fear nobody will miss it until it's gone.

The foundation of fly fishing lies in the classic confrontation between rational humans and unpredictable fish. We're fascinated with the things fish do that we can't explain. Or at least we used to be – but fallout from the information explosion is settling quickly on our sport and our fascination has been replaced by demands for facts – facts that will ensure our success in catching the fish.

We now know about (or can find out about) everything from behavioural drift of aquatic insects to modulus of elasticity in graphite. An up-to-date, new-age fly guy isn't really with it unless he can quote the pH and trout population data from trendy rivers like the Bighorn and the Green. Learning and understanding have always been important in fly fishing but lately they've come with a high cost. We've dissected our sport to death and become single-mindedly obsessed with catching the fish. And along the way we've diluted the mystery and lost respect for the unpredictable nature of our quarry.

I also worry about the latest generation of fly fishers. It seems they know where their sport is going, but they don't know where it came from. Technology and information have produced a group of fly-fishing wizards who can cast a hundred feet, match microscopic midge hatches, and tie streamers that even smell like the correct baitfish, but who don't know Robert Traver from Bryan Adams. These guys will be fly fishing's leaders in a few years, but their experience lacks a fundamental connection to the sport's Golden Age. Back then we didn't have graphite, fluorocarbon and Gore-Tex, but we did have A.J. McClane, Joe Brooks, and Ernie Schwiebert, exploring, thinking, and writing about the sport.

Fly fishing used to be a funky blend of tradition and technology, but lately the tradition side has taken a beating. We're losing our sense of heritage and without it the soul of the sport will wither and croak.

If blame is to be assigned in these matters, I plead guilty. I've introduced many people to the sport and surely have emphasized information and instruction at the expense of history and tradition. I don't have any perfect solutions, but maybe this will help: Let's take it upon ourselves, those of us who remember fly fishing as a simpler, less cluttered sport, to not only teach newcomers about the hard strategies and precise tactics, but also about the winsome traditions and compelling mysteries of fly fishing.

Let's show them things that the magazines and videos always leave out – the importance of a good repertoire of country coffee shops and bakeries on the way to the streams for instance, and the pleasure of knowing the names of the wildflowers as well as the mayflies. I'm not suggesting we abandon technology and preach silk lines and gut leaders; I am suggesting we include a bit of history with our technology. Let's not let anyone get away with thinking fly fishing is simply a clever way to catch a fish.

CHAPTER 3

Fly-Fishing Etiquette

1996

Etiquette: *the forms, manners, etc. conventionally accepted or required in society, a profession etc. (Webster's New World Dictionary)*

I parked the truck and three of us walked a few hundred yards to the river, hoping to have a stretch of water to ourselves. Lynda and Joe went upstream; I went down a bit and crossed the stream to work up the opposite side. When we had been fishing about five minutes, a truck drove up along the river on my side, passed me and parked near the head of the pool I was fishing. Three guys with lots of gear jumped out and waded into the river, trying to appear casual, but with body language that showed they wanted to get to the "good water" before I did. I got out of the river and walked upstream past them, thinking I'd leave that pool to them if it was that important. When they realized I wasn't going to hang around, they got out of the water and also began walking upstream. I recommenced fishing a few hundred yards farther up. They walked past me to the next pool and got in the water, whereupon one guy began working his way downstream, directly toward me. I was now surrounded and had no choice but to force a confrontation or gather my companions and leave. As we passed our new fishing partners' vehicle on the way back to ours, I noted the local plates and resisted the temptation to let the air out of the tires. I probably should have left a note on the windshield. Something like, "Your plan worked. You've driven us away. Happy fishing."

Fly-fishing etiquette is largely a question of how much space to give the other guy. The best way to answer the question is often simply to ask it. You can check with the other fisherman to find out where he plans to fish, and ask if it's okay if you take the other side of the creek. But of course that's like asking for directions when your spouse thinks you're lost, and most of us won't do it. The other solution comes through application of the Golden Rule. If you were the other guy, how much space would you like to have?

The "how much space" question is more complicated than you might think because expectations are different in different places. I recently returned from a popular spring creek in Montana. There is about a half-mile of this small creek available to fly fishers and the landowner charges an access fee and allows a maximum of six people to fish each day. Here nobody expects to have 300 or 400 yards of water to themselves, and as long as you're more than a few casts away from the other guy, you won't be bothering him.

You can fish quite close to other anglers in these kinds of places, but another rule that pops up is the "don't hog the good spot" rule. This can mean "don't stay there all day," but even if people adhere to this, there is often a subtle race to get to the good spots first. If several fishermen arrive at the parking lot about the same time they'll begin a cordial discussion about what the day might bring. But watch carefully and you'll notice that though they go to great lengths to create the impression of nonchalance, other things tell the real story. For instance, one guy might choose to string his rod later, after he's down the creek a ways. Another guy might not bother with a small detail like tying his wading shoes before traipsing off along the stream. Nobody will admit it, but the race is on.

There are also other more subtle issues of etiquette. One is the "no gloating" rule that's especially important at boat ramps where fly fishers finish float trips. I learned this from an outfitter who told me that he instructs all his guides to keep the conversation to general topics when they encounter other fishermen or guides at the end of the day. No discussion about numbers or size of fish, no talk about how they "slammed 'em today," even if an open shot at a competitor is available. This is good advice because everybody who's fished any amount has been on both sides of these things and nobody likes to be humiliated.

The sport of fly fishing has a great intrinsic freedom. Aside from obeying government regulations, a participant is free to do it the way he wants. If that means fishing a dry fly as a dropper off a Clouser Minnow, that's fine.

If it means making 500 casts into the same pocket behind a boulder, that's fine too.

But as great and fundamental as this freedom is, it also allows for inconsiderate behaviour in the company of other anglers. Other sports have rules about this—golfers know they can't play too slow or too fast or talk too loud, skiers know they have to line up politely at the lift—but fly fishing doesn't. Most of fly fishing's rules are the unwritten kind. This means that if somebody behaves impolitely on a trout stream, he's probably going to get away with it. But that's still no justification for bad manners.

CHAPTER 4

Mistakes

1989, 1995

It was late spring in west-central Alberta and a small foothill stream had been treating me well. There were a few stoneflies and March Brown mayflies around, so I fished my way up the creek with dries, catching a fish here and there in a pretty casual manner. After lunch and a nap on the bank, I took the dry fly off, replaced it with a big Woolly Bugger and started fishing my way back to the truck. I moved quickly, casting as I walked, trying to swim the Bugger once through each deep slot and juicy pocket.

I had caught a few average-sized fish on the Bugger when I made a cast into the slack water behind a midstream boulder. I made half of the first strip of the fly line when the fly stopped in a churning swirl behind the rock. A massive brown trout broke the surface, then broke my leader. It happened in slow motion and gave me the same immediate sense of helplessness I get when I've just driven my truck into a mud hole a little too deep.

My mistake was made right after lunch. When I switched to the streamer, I didn't switch to a heavier leader even though I know a big fly demands one. I wasn't expecting a big fish, you see, so I didn't bother to change the leader. I make plenty of mistakes through honest ignorance and I can more or less accept those, but when my excuse is nothing more than plain laziness, it really grinds me.

The biggest mistake many fly fishers make is to fail to treat the fish as a wild animal. New anglers often begin their assault on a stream by walking up to the edge of the water or wading right in to see if the fish are home. Trout are wary critters and the sight of a predator, human or otherwise, spoils their appetite in a hurry. Rule number one: If you frighten the fish, you can't catch the fish. You have to approach the water carefully and stay out of the fish's sight.

One of the few things of which you can be certain in fishing is that the conditions will change. Water temperature, water level, weather and the fish's predominant food items are constantly shifting. The angler should also change to adapt to the current conditions but too often he doesn't. A long-time fly fisher explains to his rookie friend that this sport is a cerebral game requiring an acute understanding of the quarry and a logical approach to problem solving. He then excuses himself and begins fishing with a fly that represents something the fish haven't seen in eight months. Many, or even most fly anglers get stuck in the rut of familiarity. They go to the same places and fish the same flies and methods whether it's logical or not, and then they wonder why the fishing is lousy.

You can always spot these guys. They're the ones complaining that their favourite lake or stream is fished out. When they say this, I always ask them how they know. The answer usually goes something like this: "Well, I used to catch a lot of fish in such and such a spot with such and such a fly, but last time I was there I didn't have a touch." There's some interesting logic at work here: I can't catch them; therefore, they aren't there. To be fair, there can be problems with populations of fish in a lake or stream, but I'd need to hear that from a biologist, not a fisherman. Most often the conditions have simply changed. The fish may have moved or may be feeding on different things or at different times of day. The fisherman should expect these changes and should observe the water closely so he'll be able to keep up.

We make another big mistake when we ignore the advice of local anglers. This happens more often than you'd think, and it drives professional guides crazy. Somebody hires a guide to help him catch fish, and then refuses to get value for the money he's spending. Some guys apparently feel they're paying for the opportunity to show the guide how to fish his own water. Traveling fishermen – more so traveling fly fishermen – sometimes have a funny attitude toward local anglers. They act as if the locals are uneducated country bumpkins who can't possibly know as much as sophisticated world travellers like themselves. The real experts know better.

I once guided Lefty Kreh, perhaps the most famous fly fisherman of his day. After we'd been fishing a little while he said, "Okay, take half an hour and tell me everything I'm doing wrong." This caught me by surprise, for I was about to ask him the same question. He went on to say that he believed a local fisherman would nearly always do better than a visitor, even if the

visitor was a superior angler overall. This is true because the most important factor in successful angling is knowing the water. Only by spending a lot of time on a piece of water does an angler come to understand the idiosyncrasies that make that fishery unique. If you can fish with or get advice from someone who knows the water better than you, do it.

Another mistake that haunts all of us is a lack of concentration. Most of us pay attention to what we're doing when the fishing is good, but let up a little when things slow down. We have to remind ourselves that anytime our line is in the water we're fishing, whether we're ready or not. Fish have a way of taking the fly just as we stop to light a cigar or scratch our nose or look up at a bird flying over the stream. The most successful fishermen are almost fierce in their concentration. Some even find it difficult to fish and talk at the same time. I'm not advocating this for everyone, but it might help to keep it in mind. I occasionally fish with a friend who's a relatively infrequent angler. He likes to fish, but hasn't let it dominate his life quite the way I have mine. Yet he does better than many people who fish three times as often, simply because he maintains his concentration and pays attention to what he's doing. When a fish takes his fly, he's ready.

I can't think about fishing mistakes without addressing the dull hook routine. I have mastered this through years of practice, but nearly all fly fishers are capable of it even if they won't admit it. Here's how it usually works: You're getting plenty of strikes but no hook-ups and after awhile you decide to have a look at the fly. You note with consternation that the hook has a dull or broken point and then realize it's probably been that way since you hit a rock on a backcast three hours ago. A bright person would have checked the fly the first time it failed to stick, but I guess that would be asking too much.

You can see a lot of mistakes coming if you pay attention out there, but most of us believe we're immune to temporary stupidity. Most of us are wrong.

CHAPTER 5

2005

A few days ago I fished my home river with a long-time fishing companion. We walked the river for a few hours, looking for risers. While we were sitting on the bank waiting for bugs to hatch and fish to feed, several driftboats of fly fishermen went by us, every rod rigged with what looked like a fluorescent easter-egg on the leader. This prompted my friend's observation that nymphs and indicators seem to be taking over the fly-fishing world these days.

It's not quite that simple, of course, but there certainly seems to have been a paradigm shift. Not many years ago nymphing was considered the most difficult method of catching trout in streams, requiring Yoda-like understanding of river currents and a proverbial "sixth sense" to detect strikes. While many people were intimidated by this, the idea appealed to me so I worked at it and learned to nymph fish, eventually becoming something of an advocate for it. I taught nymphing, trying to help people overcome the perceived difficulties and nymphing's inherent Catch 22 which says that to catch fish on nymphs you need confidence in the method, yet to achieve confidence you must catch fish.

But that was before pingpong ball-sized, glow-in-the-dark, air-filled strike indicators, before tungsten bead-head nymphs, and before the San Juan Worm. These things have made nymph fishing easier and more effective, and have pushed the pendulum in the other direction. On some rivers, nymph fishing is so popular that few people fish any other way. There's no denying the fact that the development of effective nymphing tackle and technique has helped many new fly fishers catch trout they otherwise wouldn't find. That's good. What's bad is the fact that the reliability of this method has stalled some of these people's development in the sport. The fly fishers I teach today are more likely to be intimidated by dry-fly fishing than by nymphing. On several occasions I've been told, "I don't mess with dries or streamers much because I know I can catch fish on nymphs."

I won't go so far as to say that nymph-and-indicator fishing is not fly fishing, or that it is somehow unethical, nor will I suggest that people shouldn't do it. I will say that as nymph-and-indicator fishing has increased, other fly-fishing skills have decreased, and I believe that's unfortunate. Notable among these skills is the formerly elegant art of fly casting. In the old days, people started with dry flies and at some point later added nymphing to their bag of tricks. This meant that the first skill they learned was conventional fly casting, which is the foundation of dry-fly fishing. Today though, many people begin with nymphs, quickly mastering the gawky technique required to throw weighted flies and indicators. They catch fish this way and never move to dry-fly fishing and the good casting it requires. No longer a graceful *swish*, *swish*, *swish*, fly casting today is more often an ungainly *flop*, *flop*, *splat*. Other casualties of this trend are the things we used to call stream-craft: observation, hatch-matching, stealth.

It's not only dry-fly fishing and streamer fishing that are being ignored. Other nymphing methods, like shallow-water nymphing, short-line nymphing, and nymphing without indicators, are disappearing too. The late Charles Brooks wrote an entire book about nymph fishing, describing in detail a dozen or more methods, none of which called for a strike indicator.

I think the real question is why this trend bothers me. Though there are

more people on the streams these days, I have less competition because few of them are doing what I like to do. This should make me happy, and on the day of a great hatch it does. But in the big picture it troubles me because my altruistic side believes that fly fishers should never stop learning. In some cases today it seems that catching fish is taking precedence over learning. If it's simply about catching fish, there is no need to use fly tackle in the first place. There are more efficient ways of accomplishing the task. I'm not trying to talk people out of fishing with nymphs and indicators; I am trying to talk them into viewing it as one method instead of the only method.

There is a short, well-worn trail that leads to simply catching fish with a fly rod, and a longer, more winding path that leads to learning how to fly fish. Strange it is that success on the former can prevent travel on the latter.

CHAPTER 6

Maturing as a Fly Fisherman

1981

I went fishing twice this week, and the experiences were as different as a sculpin is from a midge. The first day I went to an area that I cover daily in my guiding business, hoping to hit the *Tricorythodes* spinner-fall that has been buffaloing so many clients recently. When I arrived, there were several good fish working despite a slight breeze ruffling the surface of the water. I started fishing and fairly quickly hooked a rainbow large enough to break my tippet. I tied on another fly and moved up a couple of steps to work on the next fish. The breeze was becoming more noticeable and it wasn't long before it was strong enough to help me put down a couple of nice fish. Then as the swarming spinners rode the wind into the grain fields away from the river, the rest of the fish stopped rising. I sloshed out of the water, frustrated to the point of being depressed. I seldom fish alone during a guiding season and this was a day I had been counting on to sate my building desire to "catch 'em all." But I felt worse after fishing than I did before. This is what worried me. Fishing is supposed to calm me and make me feel better. Why hadn't it?

Today I went to a different area on the same river, an area where I first fished this river many years ago. It is water with which I am familiar, yet not intimately so. Again I was determined, but today I was determined to enjoy myself and the river regardless of whether I caught or even saw fish. I reminded myself that "fishing" and "catching 'em all" are separate pursuits and only rarely simultaneous.

As I started to walk upstream towards a favourite stretch of slow water, my mind, busy with memories of big fish, was suddenly struck again by the beauty of the place at this time of year. The golden poplar leaves (about half in the trees and half on the ground), the dark blue-green spruce, and the pale October sky always conspire to make the river look deliciously alive. Each landmark I passed reminded me of a past triumph or failure, and gradually I regained the familiar smell and feel of the area.

When I got to the long, slow water stretch, there were several small fish rising sporadically to what I call the "odds and ends" hatch. I fished my way slowly upstream, taking a couple of hours to cover a quarter of a mile. I caught a number of the small fish, saw no large ones, and had a great time.

What was the difference between the two days? Several things, but most notably my attitude. The first day my concern was entirely with fish and I felt cheated when it didn't turn out perfectly. Part of the problem was familiarity. I see this water everyday, and perhaps familiarity had bred, in this case, blindness to all but the fish. To enjoy fishing every time out (not a bad goal for a fly fisherman), you must be prepared to accept and deal with the circumstances that face you. On the first day, although I felt that the river and fate had let me down, in fact I had let the river down. A river can have its famed sedative effect only when you approach it with respect for its moods.

I learned something this week, but it didn't have anything to do with catching fish – it had to do with something far more important: fishing, and enjoying it.

CHAPTER 7

Further Thoughts on Catch-and-Release

2007

Many fly fishers have long considered no-kill fishing the saviour of our sport, and in many ways it has been exactly that, but there are some aspects of it that have come to trouble me lately. But first some perspective. How did catch-and-release fishing come to be?

In the beginning, fishing was simply one way of procuring food, along with hunting and the gathering of edible plants. But as we all know, fishing today is much more than that. So when and how did it change? According to Roderick Haig-Brown, it changed when "the first man sneaked away to the creek when the tribe did not really need fish." This guy went fishing for two reasons – to get some grub and to have some fun. Though he didn't need the fish, he probably ate them, because that's what you did, and this man's family may have become a little tired of fish dinners. The element of entertainment in his excursions was the seed of what we have come to call "sport." For generations since, fishing has been both a means of procuring food and a way of participating in sport.

When I was a teenager, I was enthralled by a fly-fishing book called *Trout*, written by Ray Bergman, in which the author spoke of releasing fish excess to his needs. This idea was seen as unusual and even revolutionary when the book was published in 1938. Subsequently Bergman, Lee Wulff and others promoted this idea, teaching anglers that it was not necessary to kill all the fish they caught. At this stage catch-and-release was primarily a logical way of abjuring greed and avoiding waste.

As populations grew and fishing became more popular, over-harvest became a problem on some favoured waters. That's when somebody had the idea of using catch-and-release as a management tool to protect fish stocks from over-harvest, and in a few places like Yellowstone Park, no-kill fishing became a regulation. Its purpose was to preserve the fish population while still allowing people to fish for them. It thereby acknowledged and served two ideals – the tradition of fishing for sport, and the need to preserve the fish.

The idea developed further when some fly fishers realized that it was not necessary to kill any of the fish they caught, regardless of what the regulations required. For them there was greater value in the enjoyment of catching the fish than in possessing the fish afterwards. At this point catch-and-release became a philosophy. So far, so good.

Fly fishing has continued to grow and many people have taken it up in the last couple of decades. Most of them love it for all the right reasons – it's fun, healthy, exhilarating, challenging, and it occurs in the most beautiful of settings. It is significant that many of these converts to fly-fishing have bypassed the first stage of the journey – the stage that includes catching, killing, and eating the fish – and proceeded directly to catch-and-release. This is not necessarily bad, but it troubles me that I'm meeting an increasing number of fly fishers today who believe catch-and-release should be the rule for all fishing everywhere.

This is the point at which we sit today, and it is the point at which things begin to run amuck. We've taken an idea, used it as a tool, nurtured it into a philosophy, and allowed it to become something approaching a religion.

So what's wrong with that?

What's wrong first is that the cart is quite a distance ahead of the horse. Catch-and-release has sometimes become the objective itself, rather than a tool to reach an objective. You hear the call often – "We need more no-kill regulations. The fishing would be better if we could just get no-kill regs." This is like believing insulin cures all illnesses. Insulin is a wonderful treatment in the right circumstance, but disastrous in the wrong one. Catch-and-release works the same way. It is the cure for some of the illnesses that afflict some of our fisheries, but it is not the cure for all illnesses in all places and can do harm if applied where there is no illness.

Forgetting for a moment what catch-and-release fishing does for the fish, it's interesting what some people think catch-and-release fishing does for them. There are those who apparently believe they are better human beings because they release all the fish they catch. But hold on a minute. Releasing a fish you catch is not a particularly noble act. It's pragmatic perhaps, but not noble.

I recently ran across a fine essay by the novelist, poet, fly fisher and hunter, Jim Harrision. Harrison is the author of *Legends of the Fall*, among other works. In his essay are several heavy quotes about fishing in general and catch-and-release fishing in particular, including this one: "Probably 99% of the fish I've caught in my adult life were released. I don't say released unharmed, as a creature's struggle for life is indubitably harmful to it. We should avoid a mandarin feeling of virtue in this matter. Catch-and-release is sensible, which shouldn't be confused with virtuous."

Sensible, but not virtuous. That's the way we should view catch-and-release fishing. It can be a regulatory tool, a philosophy, but never a religion.

My second objection to the deification of catch-and-release comes from a fear of the future. Our sport is coming under increasing attack from the animal rights folks. Some anglers used to think that the practice of releasing the fish we catch would insulate us from groups like People for the Ethical Treatment of Animals (PETA). That is proving to be incorrect, and in fact our love affair with catch-and-release is precisely what is drawing the attention of these groups. They consider catching and releasing fish despicable, an act significantly worse than killing the fish and eating it. (You can find more about this on the PETA website, which is called Fishing Hurts.) Some anglers say this is not a major worry because the animal rights movement represents only a small, radical, fringe element of society. That much is

probably true. But I believe our problems will be worst not when the animal rights fanatics tell us that catch-and-release fishing is cruel, but when "normal" people start to tell us that. Our downfall may not come from the animal rights movement at all, but rather from our own inability to explain catch-and-release to the rational, reasonable segment of society. This is a segment for which some high profile voices have begun to speak. Do the names Jacques Cousteau and David Suzuki ring any bells? To quote the old *Pogo* comic strip, "We have seen the enemy and it's us."

So what do we do? First, we must dispense with the idea that it's wrong to kill and eat a fish. This wasn't a problem in the old days because most fishermen were also hunters, but regrettably that is less frequently the case today. It is regrettable because fishing is a sister - a blood-sister - to hunting. You don't have to kill and eat the fish you catch, but if you think it's wrong to do so, you probably shouldn't be fishing. Jim Harrison again: "This (fishing) is a blood sport and if you want a politically correct afterglow you should return to golf. Eating some wild trout now-and-then will serve to remind you that they are not toys put in the river for the exercise of your

expensive equipment." Ouch.

Second, we must think carefully about how we present catch-and-release to the people in the middle of the spectrum of opinion – those who are neither anglers nor animal rights supporters. If these people see catch-and-release fishing as a sport pulled out of the air, simply invented one day like baseball, it will be correctly viewed as absurd. Playing with, traumatizing, and stressing wild animals for entertainment, without dignifying them by killing and eating them? Absurd, indeed. So how should we explain no-kill fishing? We should say that it evolved through a logical sequence of events with the purpose of allowing fishing while preserving fish populations. We should say that in some places it is the best option available, the others being over-harvest of fish by angling or the elimination of fishing altogether. When it's presented this way most people will see the logic. But to try to justify it on moral grounds is to step into quicksand with both feet. We cannot present catch-and-release as something we do because we like to catch fish but don't think it's right to kill them. We anglers must view catch-and-release as a management tool, and we must present it as such to non-anglers.

Where to from here? Let's embrace catch-and-release for what it is – a tool with which something is built or repaired; the means but never the objective. Let's not presume that it is the correct medicine for all illnesses, and let's never allow it to become a religion. Catch-and-release regulations should be implemented with sound logic and clear understanding of the management objectives. In this regard, we should look to the scientists for information. They deal in facts while anglers' currency is emotion and "gut feelings." When no-kill regulations are proposed, we should ask the biologists what affect the regulations will have on the fishery. If they are the right tool for the job, we must work hard to see that they are put in place. If they are not, we must resist the temptation to implement them for reasons of misplaced morality.

Let's put the horse back in front of the cart.

CHAPTER 8

Night Fishing

1999

There are a lot of things about fly fishing that might be considered strange, but none any stranger than the practice of fly fishing at night. Oh, I've read the magazine stories (and there's even a whole book on night fishing, written by an otherwise competent and sane man), and I know that the really big fish come out after dark along with the truly committed fishermen, those wearing miner's headlamps and using big rods to launch giant streamers and mouse imitations into the gloom.

My night-fishing experience is pretty limited, and I'm thankful for those kinds of small mercies. However, I was talked into a dose of it one time by a couple of well-meaning if somewhat eccentric friends. We had a nap in the evening when we would have normally been fishing and went to the river about 11 pm. We rowed a boat across the river and spread ourselves out along a deep run. We fished big streamers that "move lots of water" just like the books said we should. I remembered to use a heavy tippet, to wade carefully and even to take along a flashlight and bug spray. After about 20 minutes of working the water carefully, I decided to try something different. I reeled in, fumbled to find the end of my fly line and felt my way down the leader to where my streamer was supposed to be. It was missing, and I had no idea where it had gone, nor how long I'd been without it.

I lit a match so I could see to find my miniature flashlight, which I was pretty sure was hiding in the top pocket of my vest. In the process, I set my eyebrows on fire. Eventually I found the light, turned it on, held it in my teeth and got a new fly tied on about the same time the batteries gave out and saliva began to drip onto the back of my hand. Once I got things organized, I continued working my way down the run, trying to swim the fly seductively through where I thought the best water was. About 20 minutes later, I decided to change flies again, and again I discovered that I had no fly to change, and no idea where it had gone nor how long it had been absent. Maybe I burned it up or fried my tippet with the match. This time, after reeling up, I had the best idea of the night. I thrashed my way back into the bushes and took a nap while my friends got this out of their system.

I have another friend who actually fishes at night with some regularity. He fishes one spot only - a pool on his home stream he naturally calls the "night hole" - and only after he's had a couple of martinis. He says the idea doesn't appeal much until then. Most of his stories are of filled waders, broken tippets, and foul-hooked bats.

Once in a while I find myself on a trout stream after dark, but I don't count this as real night fishing because it's just an extended session of day fishing. Yet even this isn't very satisfying, for when I do catch a nice fish, I can't admire it or take its picture properly.

Fly fishing at night seems a little like waltzing by yourself. You can make all the right moves, but something important is still missing. I'm sure night fishing is productive and maybe even fun at times. What I'm not sure of is how much of that kind of fun I can stand. I felt a jolt of anxiety the other day when a friend suggested I meet him on his water some night when there's a full moon. I didn't come up with much of an excuse, but I'm counting on him forgetting he brought it up. If you want to try this sometime, by all means go ahead, just don't invite me okay?

CHAPTER 9

The Other Guy

2006

At the risk of dumping another "yearning for the good old days" rant on you, I have to tell you of a fly-fishing trend that I find pretty funny. When two fly fishers run into each other on the water these days, they'll probably both pretend the other guy doesn't exist. They might pass each other on a path along a trout stream without even making eye contact. It's as if our trout waters have become the outdoors' equivalent of a subway car or an elevator. You see the other guy, you know the other guy sees you, but you don't look up and you certainly don't do anything as rash as initiating a conversation. Both guys play this game, but they both have to know that it's pretty silly.

Of course I understand where this has come from. There are more people on the water these days, especially on our best (read "most crowded") waters, and I know that to engage every angler you meet in such places would turn your day in to a chat session instead of a fishing trip. I also understand that when you meet me on a stream it might mean that I've appeared in a place where you didn't want me to appear, maybe in a place you thought nobody else knew about. And, it might mean that I've just fished the water you've been daydreaming about all week.

I also understand, through experience, that a certain awkwardness can develop during these unplanned encounters. If Angler A has had poor fishing, he's not inclined to discuss it with Angler B, especially if Angler B approaches with a huge smile, suggesting that he, on the other hand, has had a banner day. Fair enough, but even so doesn't it strike you as a bit odd when people who so obviously share the same interest (and on this occasion the same location) try so hard to ignore each other?

It wasn't always like this. Fly fishers used to share a common bond—the brotherhood of the long rod, the fraternity of the fly-fishing community—all that camaraderie stuff that included everything but a secret handshake. Then there is the cliched but true story of the Good Samaritan fly fisher who cuts off the fly that is working and gives it to a frustrated rookie. I made a stab at this myself the other day when I ran into a gentleman older than I who was having trouble threading a tiny fly onto his tippet. My attempt fizzled because I couldn't get it threaded either, but I think he appreciated the thought.

I'm not suggesting you turn every stranger you meet on the water into your bosom-buddy/fishing partner for the day, but aside from the courtesy perspective it makes sense to say howdy for practical reasons. At the very least, you might learn something. You might find out how far up the river the other guy has fished or intends to fish, or what method he used that worked or didn't work.

So if you run into a guy on your stream who seems a little too insistent in engaging you when you don't want to be engaged, just smile and indulge him a little. It's probably me or someone like me, trying to hang onto one of the good things about fly fishing. I won't take it as far as the pranksters who ride elevators and strike up loud conversations just for their own entertainment, but I'll probably say hi and ask you how the fishing has been, even if I can tell you don't want to talk. I won't get in your way or take too much of your time, I promise.

The Why Factor

1996

As I get older, it's becoming apparent that you can spend your whole life messing around with fly fishing and still end up with more questions than answers. My most common question is "why?" and it's often directed at myself, as in, why does it take four missed strikes before I think to check if my hook is broken? (It is.) Or why, when I'm fishing late into the evening, do I cut the fly off my leader before realizing it's too dark to tie another one on?

But sometimes the why is directed at the fish, and they generally don't respond well. For instance, since they're not supposed to be feeding, why do steelhead take flies? Furthermore, why do steelhead sometimes take dry flies? Or, why does a trout carefully refuse my best dry flies and then rush eagerly up to chomp my fluorescent orange strike indicator as soon as I switch to nymphs?

A couple of recent experiences really left me scratching my head. The first was in April on the Crowsnest River. The fish sometimes rise to midges there on warm April afternoons, but this day they weren't. Fair enough, I thought, so I rigged up with a pair of size 18 nymphs on 6X tippet. I made long casts to stay out of the fish's sight. I made tuck casts so the flies would sink quickly and drift without drag. I caught no fish.

This fact alone was not especially surprising nor troubling. The trouble arrived in the form of another fisherman, whom I met on my way back to the truck at lunchtime. I tried to steer conversation away from the subject of how the fishing was so I wouldn't have to choose between being a liar or an incompetent. But the other guy quickly explained that he had been tearing up the rainbows with a San Juan Worm. A size 4 San Juan Worm, he said. I was pretty sure he was making this up, because I knew that the logical, scientific approach was to use small subtle nymphs and light tippet rather than a goofy red fly. After lunch I put on the biggest San Juan Worm in my fly box and waded out to the head of a pool to prove that it wouldn't work. On the first cast, I caught the biggest fish of my season. On the third cast I caught one only slightly smaller. So much for science. I cut off the fly and went back to the car, wondering why the fish would do this to me.

The other puzzling event took place on a small, brown trout stream. The first spot I fished was a beautiful undercut bank with thick willows hanging over. My first 10 casts there produced not one but two very nice browns on dry flies. Things were looking good. However, the next 10 casts produced zero fish, as did the next 10, the next 100 and the next 500. For three more hours, I fished with not a sniff from another trout. Then, within sight of my vehicle at the end of the day, I cast my Stimulator into a tiny pocket of foam behind a small sweeper on the far bank. An 18-inch brown ambushed it immediately. I landed this fish and then in spite of all logic cast into the same tiny pocket again. Another 18-inch brown nabbed it. I landed this fish, took a couple of photographs and put my tackle away. I was certain there was something to learn here, but didn't know what it might be. Were there only four fish in the water I fished? If so, why were two of them crammed into one tiny hole? Or, were there lots of fish there, but only four hungry ones? Had I read the water incorrectly? Had somebody fished the water ahead of me?

You're supposed to gain a little understanding from each day you spend on the water, but sometimes it seems I'm going in the other direction. Is it a cop out if I conclude that there's some stuff out there we're not supposed to understand?

CHAPTER 11

The Last Dance

2005

It's taken thirty years, but I've finally figured out that the reason I fish and hunt is to create memories. These memories play a crucial role in my life by providing sanctuary into which I can intentionally or accidentally retreat when the circumstances of the moment are troubling or are at least less interesting than fishing and hunting. Recently, I've noticed that many of the best fishing memories are created in the fertile months of September and October.

The season of autumn strikes with an assault on the senses, and does so most vigorously in the presence of water. Autumn is the aroma of weeds dead and drying on the rocks along the Bow, their sour smell mixing with the sweet scent of harvest up beyond the river breaks. It's the life-and-death scent of new snow and old salmon on B.C.'s Bulkley River. Autumn is the strange croaking call of sandhill cranes passing so high that you can't find them in a cloudless sky.

Have you noticed that the light is different in the fall? It carries a warm, amber undertone and gives the outdoor world a rich glow that isn't there earlier in the summer. I have a favourite camping spot near the south end of Alberta's Forestry Trunk Road, and I love driving south from the trailer on sharp October mornings when the sun illuminates the yellow aspens along the road and the stoic peaks of the Flathead Range across the valley.

In fall the days are shorter, the nights are cooler, and the best fishing is compressed into a few hours at the warmest part of the day. When I was young and impatient, this irritated me because I liked to start early and stay late and wanted to have good fishing the whole time. But lately I'm less troubled by nature's autumn timetable and have come to appreciate the benefits of the shorter days. I now find myself looking forward to the long evenings when a good meal, a campfire, and a cigar will close the day perfectly.

While fall is a great time to fish almost anywhere, for me it is best spent in familiar territory. If I've been diligent and committed to the task, my exploratory trips will be done by the time September arrives, and I'll be drawn to close the season on my home water. You should always save the last dance for your spouse.

I once had a fly-shop discussion about autumn with a fellow angler. Ted is as keen to fish as I am, and we agree on many things but not on the subject of fishing in the fall. Ted hates it. He hates it because of what it means. He hates the thought of the fishing coming to an end and being replaced by an off season that lasts five or six months. It's a perfectly valid point of view, but nonetheless not one I share.

To me the fall is the climax of the fishing season. Everything I like about fly fishing is magnified through the golden lens of autumn. The water conditions are good, the weather is good, the fishing is good. Like Ted, I know it means that a special time of year is coming to an end, but I'm okay with that. It took awhile before I could admit it, but I now believe that it's acceptable, and in an odd way maybe even beneficial to stop fishing for a while. Would it make it any better if we could do it all the time? When I was younger, I was sure it would, and I did my best to prove it. But I now appreciate the wisdom of the book of *Ecclesiastes*, which says "There is a time for everything, and a season for every activity under heaven: a time to be born and a time to die, a time to plant and a time to uproot..." To which I'll add a humble paraphrase: A time to cast and a time to refrain from casting. You have to put the fishing season to bed at some point. It really is good to have an off-season, isn't it? *Isn't it?*

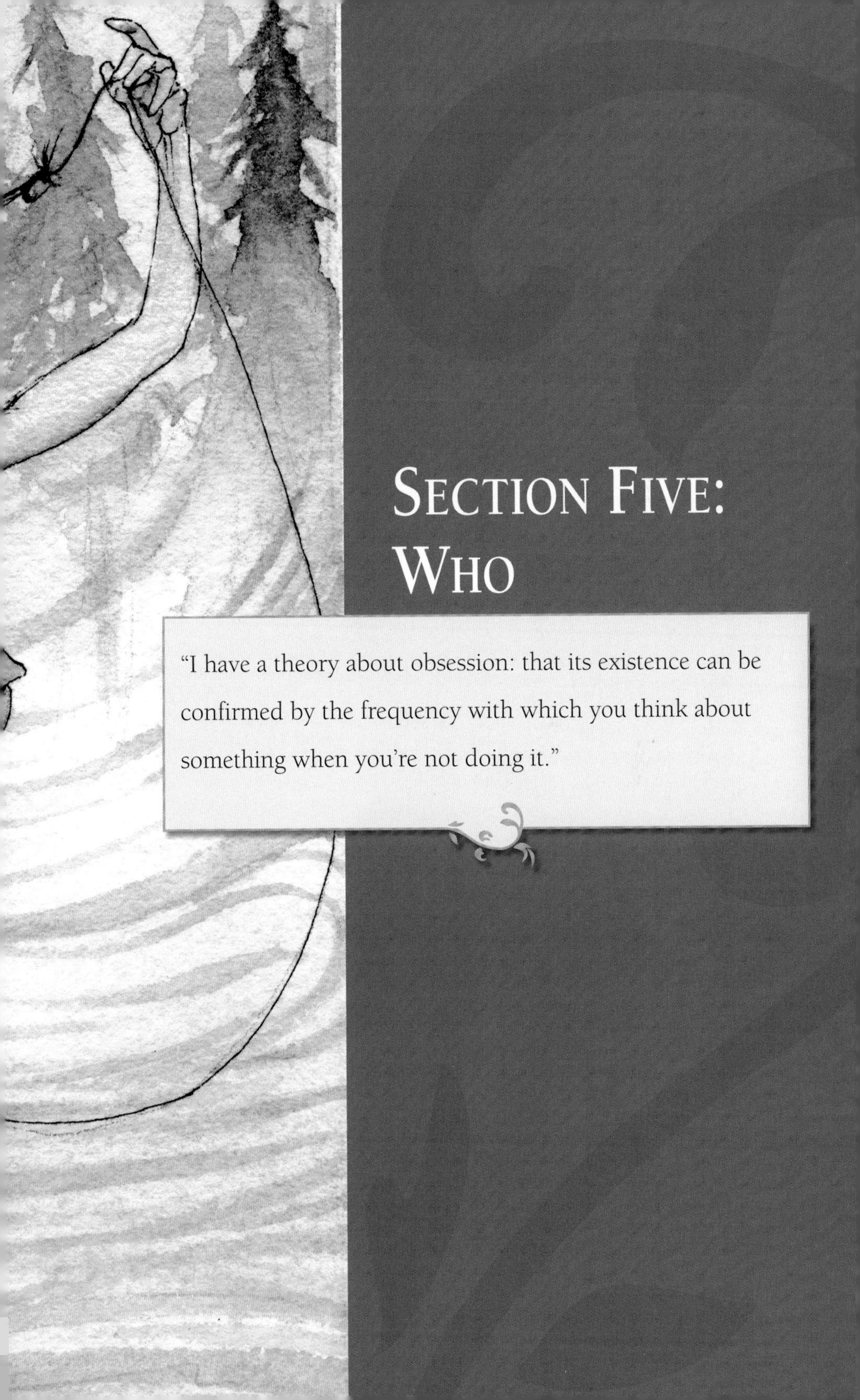

Section Five: Who

"I have a theory about obsession: that its existence can be confirmed by the frequency with which you think about something when you're not doing it."

CHAPTER 1

Ditching the Script

1996

He's a fly-fishing guide, but you won't find him in a slick fishing video or TV show. He doesn't have a promotional brochure, he doesn't advertise in the fishing magazines and he isn't endorsed by the New Zealand Department of Tourism. In fact you might not find him at all unless you care to crawl through the backcountry scrub of Canterbury or Westland and keep an eye out for a red Land Rover piloted by a pony-tailed, ear-ringed guy with a black goatee and a cat-that-swallowed-the-canary smile. It's not that Bob Vaile doesn't want clients – he just wants a small number of the right clients.

And in that regard Vaile approaches things a little – well, a little differently than most guides. He screens potential customers much the way fishermen usually screen outfitters. It's a kind of audition. He would rather turn down business than end up stuck in the bush with the wrong person. When I tell him about someone who's interested in hiring him, he begins the questions: "Can he cast? Can he walk all day? Does he understand what we're really after out there?" And, now that my wife and I have spent three weeks in Bob Vaile's care, I'm compelled to add a question of my own: "Does the fisherman have a sense of humour?" He will surely need it.

Bob Vaile loves to laugh. He sees fishing as entertainment and believes that the entertainment is always there if we're smart enough to find it. No one works harder to put a good sneak on a big trout, but no one laughs harder when the whole scheme deteriorates into slapstick.

Vaile took a rather circuitous route into his guiding career. Born in Toronto, the son of a prominent eye surgeon, he spent six weeks in the History Department of the University of Toronto in the 1970s before dropping out and going to work in a dress factory.

After leaving Toronto in the '70s Vaile moved to Alberta, receiving a Bachelor of Commerce degree from the University of Calgary in 1983. He then went to work for the Calgary office of a large international accounting firm, eventually becoming a chartered accountant in 1987. While in Alberta, he discovered his sense of comfort in the high country and his love of fly fishing.

It was while he was in his accounting phase that I first met Bob Vaile. He came regularly into my fly shop to buy tackle. He was young, baby-faced, and "upwardly mobile." He bought a lot of flies. His face usually carried an intense smile, and he talked a lot. Some would have called him a yuppie. I didn't know what to call him, but it was impossible not to notice the extra jolt of passion that fueled his attack on fishing in particular and life in general. In the late '80s, he served a term as national treasurer of Trout Unlimited Canada.

Under the weight of a failed marriage, he took a leave of absence from his practise in 1988 and began his "Year of Fly Fishing the World," during which he spent time in British Columbia and Washington state chasing steelhead, and in Montana, Christmas Island, Tasmania, Australia, and New Zealand. In between these trips he guided fishermen on Alberta's Bow River, quickly developing a reputation as the most entertaining guide on the river.

When he returned from his fly-fishing tour in 1989, minus the Bay Street suit, but equipped with new goatee, ponytail, earring and attitude, he sold his house in Canada, packed up his stuff and found himself an accounting job in Christchurch. Once settled there, he spent his weekends deep in the back country – hiking (which the Kiwis call "tramping"), hunting, climbing, rafting and most especially learning to fish for the big brown trout that haunt South Island streams.

By June 1991 the sagging New Zealand economy presented him with the likelihood of a layoff, and rather than accept it he elected to retire. Thus began his "Year of No Fixed Address" during which he explored more of the hidden nooks and crannies of the South Island, auditioning possible locations from which to headquarter his days.

He finally selected as his base a small village in the southern Alps called Arthur's Pass. How small? Small enough that letters addressed "Bob, Arthur's Pass, NZ" find him easily. (But then the Arthur's Pass post office is only open for a half hour each day.) With his possessions pared down to little beyond fishing and hunting gear, books and CDs, and his living expenses at a minimum, he was free to develop a lifestyle that most of his jealous (and working) Canadian friends would both admire and hate him for. He spent virtually all his time in the back country, exploring trout streams, hunting deer, pigs, goats and chamois, meeting and befriending sheep farmers and itinerant anglers. In short, he adopted a life most of us fantasize about but lack the jam to try.

Vaile now guides fly anglers on a very limited basis, and he has learned his craft well. A New Zealand guide not only does what every guide must – that is, make profitable use of the client's abilities while compensating for his deficiencies, but he must also outright find the guy a fish. The name of the game in New Zealand is sight fishing – hunting for and spotting a fish before casting. Occasionally the fish are easy to spot – dark shapes swaying over pale gravel, sticking out, as Bob would say "like dog's balls." More often though, they're close to impossible for an untrained eye to see. One afternoon when we're walking and looking, Vaile slows as though the air is getting stiff, stops, stares into the water and concentrates, as if he can create a fish by trying hard. Finally he says, "I've got one for you. Come over here

so you can see where he is." I move slowly up behind him and look down his pointing finger into the water. I see blurry rocks. "Right there," he says, trying to point harder. "Right where?" I ask. "Hmm," he says. "Okay, just get into the water quietly and I'll direct your casts."

I do, and on about the fourth, a trout's head reaches up through a riffle to take my dry fly. Vaile cackles like a giant dwarf in a Mother Goose story while I fight the trout. It is an average brown for these streams—just short of five pounds—and after we land and release the fish, Vaile pumps my hand in congratulation, trying to create the impression that it's me who has done something well here. We both know the truth. Still, I don't want to let him off easy. "If there wasn't really a fish there you could have said I spooked one and I'd have never known the difference," I chided and then added "I think you made that fish up and then got lucky." Bob winked and said, "Yeah? Well, maybe I did."

It's no surprise that Bob Vaile also operates his guiding business in a manner different from the norm. He provides the fishing dope, the 4-wheel drive vehicle, the cooking and camping gear, and the anglers pay all expenses, including his. The nature and cost of accommodation and meals are at the clients' discretion, and they can choose anything between first rate motels and sleep-outs beside the truck.

Vaile's preference is to use the extensive system of backcountry huts available throughout the South Island. Some of these began as sheep shearer's quarters or professional deer-hunter's camps, and others were built by the government for hikers and hunters. The accommodation in a hut is minimalistic – roof, mattresses, and sink - but the setting is invariably otherworldly. There are 4-wheel drive trails to many of these huts but they are far enough out of the way that it is a rare surprise to see other anglers using them.

A day on a stream with Bob Vaile is anything but tightly focussed. After dozing off under a beech tree after lunch one day, I awaken to the realization that Bob is still talking. "The problem with politicians," he carries on from a starting point I've missed, "is that they aren't held accountable for their campaign promises. All promises should be recorded and anybody who doesn't keep them should have to forfeit a portion of his government pension." I can't think of a suitable comment, and soon give up and pretend I'm still asleep.

On the long walk back to the truck after fishing, he holds forth again: "You can learn all the common sense you need in life from three children's stories – *The Emperor's New Clothes*, *The Boy Who Cried Wolf*, and *Green Eggs and Ham*." To which my wife, catching on, replies, "Gee, Bob, what kind of flower is this?"

Seeing him walking along a clear South Island trout stream there is little to distinguish him from another Kiwi guide – camo shirt, broad-brimmed hat, hiking shorts, and backpack carried by broad shoulders and big thighs. But he has adopted more than just the Kiwi fishing uniform. He has become a New Zealand citizen and has immersed himself in his new country's culture, right down to what is perhaps the Kiwis' only questionable trait – the disgusting habit of putting a gungy paste called Marmite, which looks and tastes like used crankcase grease, on their toast every morning.

In his travels he has become friends with Kiwi farmers, many of whom have good trout streams or duck swamps on their land. One of Bob's current projects is teaching a farmer friend's young son to fly fish. He visits several times a summer and takes the boy out on the stream. Bob considers it only a slightly greater challenge that the boy is blind.

Through our whole trip I tried to figure out just what it is that sets Bob Vaile apart, for there's no doubt something is different here. Then one day, without my asking, he simply told me: "In the middle class, when you're born you're given a script. That script tells you what to do and when to do it. Graduate by 25, marry by 30, have lots of money by 40, that kind of thing. It works for some people but not for me. In 1983 I chucked out that script and began writing my own lines. You can spend your life doing what other people tell you to do, or you can make it up as you go. I prefer the latter." The fact is he is bright, educated, well read, charismatic and silly: a kind of liberal redneck; simultaneously a complete intellectual and a complete goof.

His goofy side is partly a disguise though, for his social conscience is not always suppressed and there are no sacred cows in his world. With Bob Vaile, it seems you either talk about subjects that mean nothing, or subjects that mean everything. He frequently writes letters to the Christchurch newspaper – letters containing paragraphs like this: "What about bad parenting and the freedom to have children? Maybe the state should have a say in the matter before the child is born. I submit that prospective parents should have to prove that they are capable of supporting and caring for a child before it is conceived." This one had the radio stations lining up for interviews.

After we're home from our trip, we receive letters from Bob. At the top of each, along with the East Winds Fishing Guides logo and slogan ("When the wind is in the south the beer is in the mouth, when the wind is in the east that's when you'll get the beast") is a quote from a, well, "inspirational" source – Cormac McCarthy, John Prine, Hunter S. Thompson, Mark Twain, a Maori elder, or Groucho Marx. His latest letter advises that he will be returning to Canada for a visit again this summer, accompanied, as it turns out, by a lady friend. "Hmmm," I think. The quote at the top of this letter is Audrey Hepburn to Buddy Ebsen in *Breakfast at Tiffany's:* "You mustn't give your heart to a wild thing. The more you do, the stronger they get, until they are strong enough to run into the woods or fly into a tree. And then to a higher tree, and then to the sky."

Fly Bob.

Post Script: Bob Vaile is still in New Zealand, has fathered two children (without the state's permission), and has retired from guiding.

Home Water

1996

I don't think anybody feels sorry for me when it comes to fishing, for I've certainly done my share. In fact, I've probably used up several other people's allotments of "trips of a lifetime." The memories of fishing trips are one of the most important parts of the sport for me, but lately I've been thinking more about the idea of home water.

It started recently when I spent a couple of days with my friend Bob Scammell, fishing his home stream, which is a temperamental brown trout creek in the foothills of western Alberta. Over the last 20 years or so, I've fished and hunted with Bob dozens of times. He has been both friend and mentor to me and is regarded by many as the Dean of Canadian outdoor writers.

The first day began with Bob showing me the location of a big brown trout. His directions were anything but vague: "He lives along that bank, somewhere between that willow bush and the fallen log over there." With Bob's help I caught the fish and afterward while we were admiring its gold sides and orange spots Bob said, "I haven't seen this guy since last fall. I was wondering if he was still around."

The rest of the trip went pretty much the same way – Bob predicting with great accuracy where the fish would be, what they would take, and how big they were. Some of them had names. Bob possesses the kind of understanding you simply can't get by fishing a stream once or twice, or even ten or fifteen times a year. Bob began fishing this water 30 years ago and now spends more than 50 nights a year in his cabin on its banks. It's not the only water he loves—he has favourites throughout the West and beyond—but when he's on his home creek, he never wishes he was somewhere else.

When you have a piece of home water you can afford to ease up in your single-minded pursuit of fish, and that allows you to notice some of the other things that go on around a trout stream. Bob has certainly kept track of his brown trout over the years, but he's kept track of other things too. He knows when the wild roses will bloom behind the cabin and when the stoneflies will emerge in the bouldery pool upstream. He knows when the whitetails will sneak into the hayfield across the creek to feed, and which fallen log the cock ruffed grouse will use as his drumming station. I don't know if Bob gets a bigger kick out of fooling a big trout or finding a big patch of Morel mushrooms.

One of Bob's passions is studying the correlation between the blooming of wildflowers and the hatching of aquatic insects on the stream. This began as a way to get an idea of what bugs might be around so he could have a better chance of catching a fish, but it has since become an end unto itself. Bob has been noting the hatching and blooming dates, and photographing the insects on the corresponding flowers for the last ten years or so, and the results have become a book called *The Phenological Fly*.

I'm envious of Bob because of his trout water of course, but I'm even more envious of his deep understanding of the stream and the land it flows through. Through his initial fascination with fly fishing he's attained a rare degree of intimacy with this part of this ecosystem. Fly fishing can do that for you. It can show you things you didn't know you were interested in. Sometimes it shows you things you didn't know existed.

Bob started out as most fly fishers do – as a guy with a dream of catching a big fish. But along the way he got sidetracked into a greater understanding of how the outdoor world connects with itself. And he's richer because of it.

CHAPTER 3

2005

When outdoor icon Andy Russell died in Pincher Creek, Alberta in June, 2005, the wild country got quieter. It not only lost one of its strongest voices, it lost one of its most compelling characters.

Andy was acutely aware of his calling, which was, in the words Ian Tyson used to describe the great cowboy artist, Charlie Russell, to "get 'er all down, before she goes." His twelve books, among them *Grizzly Country*, *Memoirs of a Mountain Man*, *The Life of a River*, and *The Canadian Cowboy*, are required reading for those who want to get the stories from someone who was there when they happened. Andy Russell spent more than 60 years "getting 'er all down" - on paper, on celluloid and with his voice.

He was an astute student of the outdoors and Man's interaction with it, and he came along at the perfect time. Andy Russell lived western history, beginning as a boy in the early 20th century and continuing through his life as a cowboy, outfitter, filmmaker and wilderness advocate. He was there when Alberta was young and green, and witnessed first-hand the homesteading of the southern foothills and the damming of his beloved Oldman River.

Andy Russell could be an outdoorsman's hero for any of his skills and achievements, but especially significant to me is the way he deflated the notion that environmentalists and hunters must be adversaries. He was an unapologetic hunter who possessed an extraordinary understanding of wildlife, and that combination garnered him respect from all quarters. When he spoke as a hunter, environmentalists listened. When he spoke as a conservationist, hunters listened. He embraced the role of convincing society that the two are not opposites.

Andy's life-work of recording Alberta's history and protecting its land and wildlife from the onslaught of civilization has been acknowledged repeatedly. He received four honourary university degrees and the Alberta government's Order of the Bighorn Award. The plaque honouring him with the highest distinction a civilian Canadian can receive, the Order of Canada, was hung without pomp alongside sheep and elk heads on the wall of the Hawk's Nest—a small log house he lived in near Waterton Park.

It's true that other people observe, photograph, and write about history and wildlife in the West. Some of them do it nearly as well as Andy did. His greatest gift, though, was one that few of the others possess. It's the grand and sacred gift of storytelling, which Andy learned through his life-long association with early settlers and aboriginal Albertans. Like all the best, Andy Russell was a sneaky storyteller. It's only after you've finished reading a story that you realize you've not only been entertained, you've also been taught.

My first encounter with this trait was in the library of Edmonton's Victoria Composite High School in 1967. There I found and thumbed through a copy of *Grizzly Country* when I was supposed to be studying math. I then borrowed the book and read it when I was supposed to be writing an English essay.

A few decades later when I was helping run a fly-fishing store in Calgary, Andy would occasionally come by the shop to get some flies or leaders. Every visit was accompanied by a wonderful story of a fish, a horse, or an adventure. All activity around the shop – from both customers and staff – stopped while Andy was in flight. When he was done he'd tip his big black hat, smile, and disappear around the corner like something I had imagined.

THE HAWKS
NEST

Though I grew up in the city, I have always felt a far stronger pull to things that lay outside the city. Some of this is Andy's doing, and for that I'm grateful.

The cultural roots of Alberta are not found at West Edmonton Mall or the Calgary Tower. They are found in the grass, the hills, the trees, and the sky. Like it or not, what got us here is our connection to these things. Our heritage is rural. It's my sad observation that our society at best forgets this heritage, and at worst tries to distance itself from it as though it were a source of embarrassment. Why do we do that? Other parts of the world are proud of their roots, and we should be too. Andy Russell's stories provide fine and strong antidote to this ailment and to our silly obsession with our own sophistication.

In the epilogue to his final book, *Wild Country*, Russell wrote, "All this man really needs to be happy is some rich earth to grow food, a good gun or two, a fine fishing rod, a saddle, a collection of books, and what he stands up in." Andy Russell aspired not to wealth, but to understanding. He gained understanding by observing, by doing, and by listening to those who came before. With this he left us a perfect template for achieving wisdom, and it's my earnest hope that we're smart enough to use it.

Unmatched

2006

Like most sports, ours has its celebrities, but fly fishing has only a handful that are truly larger than life. They are the groundbreakers, the ones who pursued fish with fly rods world-wide and did things no one else was doing before they started to do them.

The list of true fly-fishing giants is short, and as I see it includes Lee Wulff, Joe Brooks, A.J. McClane, Lefty Kreh, Roderick Haig-Brown, Ernest Schwiebert and perhaps no others. Time is taking these men from us, and it took one of the biggest in December, 2005, when Ernest Schwiebert died at his home in New Jersey.

Not everyone who reads this will know who Ernest Schwiebert was, for his activities were outside the fly-fishing mainstream for a number of years prior to his death, but all those who fly fish have come under his influence. He was one of the first to successfully apply a scientific approach to the imitation of trout food, as revealed in his first book, *Matching the Hatch*, which he wrote while a student at Ohio State University, and which is often considered the first fly-fishing entomology book of the modern era.

Possessing extraordinary memory and intellect, Schwiebert earned two doctorates from Princeton and worked 15 years for a Manhattan architecture firm, designing airports and military bases. Through the 1970s and '80s he was the "world's leading fly fisherman," writing prolifically in books and frequently in *Fly Fisherman* magazine. He was a charismatic and recognizable figure, and rumours of his impending arrival at a fishing lodge or a river created the same kind of stir as hearing that Arnold Palmer had booked a tee-time at the local club. This similarity was not lost on one writer, who dubbed the fans who sometimes followed Schwiebert along trout streams, "Ernie's Army."

Schwiebert brought to fly fishing and fly-fishing writing a strong element of refined culture and decorum. Many of his stories described and celebrated exotic locations and famous companions like Charles Ritz or members of the Hemmingway family. He often said as much about the wine that accompanied the streamside lunch as he did about the fishing. Much of what he did, where he did it, and the people he did it with was inaccessible to his readers, and this turned some away from his writing. And his writing style was not without its critics, many of whom frowned on his use of italics for relating dialogue. Like most people at the top of the heap, he was an easy target, and his stature provoked some jealousy among his peers. But his writing about the places, the beauty and his own insatiable love for fly fishing and all things related, was rarely equaled.

His crowning writing achievement was the publication of the two-volume book *Trout*, in 1978. It is 1745 pages long, and addresses every conceivable fly-fishing topic. If you haven't seen this book, borrow a copy from a friend or a library and take a look. Flip through chapters like "The Ancient Origins of Angling," "The Prehistory of Trout and Grayling," and "The Biosystems of Lakes and Impoundments." Then, after you understand the enormous breadth and depth of the book, note that there are no photographs, but instead hundreds of elegant pencil drawings and watercolour paintings—118 illustrations of insects and trout foods alone. Then realize that Schwiebert illustrated the book himself. Some people marvel that he worked on this book for 17 years. I marvel that it was conceived and produced by one man in one lifetime. *Trout* is a unique combination of technical brilliance and world-wide experience, shaped and underpinned by Schwiebert's unbridled passion for fly fishing.

The last words here then, are his, from *Trout*, where he answers the big question of why he fly fished: "Perhaps it is simply the beauty of fly-fishing. Such beauty is rare in the cacophony and ugliness that too often fill our lives, and trout fishing is often beautiful. Its skills are a perfect equilibrium between tradition, physical dexterity and grace, strength, logic, esthetics, our powers of observation, problem solving, perception, and the character

of our experience and knowledge. It also combines the primordial rhythms of the stalk with the chesslike puzzles of fly-hatches and fishing, echoing the blood rituals of the hunt without demanding the kill. Its subtle mixture of these ancient echoes and our increasing reverence for life make it unique."

WHO

CHAPTER 5

2003

Perhaps because she's an only child, my daughter has been subjected to an excessive amount of urging into a lifestyle of fishing and hunting. When she was born our friends made all the usual jokes, asking when she'd get her first fly rod and what size waders she needed. The friends laughed, but I didn't, probably because it was closer to the truth than anybody realized. Above my desk is a snapshot of a five month-old baby sitting on her mother's knee. Her mother is wearing waders and a fishing hat, and is sitting in a driftboat. This was not our daughter's first float trip; it was her first postnatal float trip.

We showed Deanna how to cast with a Snoopy rod and reel in the backyard when she was about four, and shortly thereafter she began reeling in fish that Lynda or I hooked at a small pond near home. When she was seven or eight, she entered the difficult stage when kids want to use a fly rod like their parents, but aren't yet strong enough to cast a fly rod. We maneuvered our way through this period by appointing her as our official fish-netter and fish-releaser, which she viewed as important jobs, and which satisfied her, more or less, until she was able to handle a fly rod on her own.

She caught her first fish with a fly rod on a rainy float trip in British Columbia when she was nine years old, and I recall clearly a few years later watching her hook, land, and release a number of cutthroats in the Elk River. A couple of years after that she stalked, hooked and landed her first big Bow River rainbow on a dry fly.

Deanna was learning things through these years, but I was too. Most important for me was the realization that it would be very easy to push too hard. Though inside I hoped she'd become the next Joan Wulff, or the first female guide on the Bow River, or at least would marry a guy who fished with dry flies and hunted with pointing dogs, I also sensed that I could drive my daughter away from fishing and hunting if I forced them upon her. Quite early I learned that every session of fishing should be accompanied by equal time for rock throwing or bug watching, and in some ways that hasn't changed much.

Last summer, when she was 16, we went on a father-and-daughter fishing trip. For two days we hiked along a brown trout stream that flows through a friend's land in the western Alberta foothills. Fishing was - well, fishing. There wasn't much activity except for a brief, but stellar episode with a good-sized brown trout and some Pale Morning Duns. We could see the fish just under the surface beside a fallen spruce tree, taking every bug that drifted over. On the third cast, Deanna's fly dropped just behind the trout. It must have heard the fly land, for it made an immediate pirouette and began to home in on the fly, coming right toward us. When the fish opened its mouth to take the fly, it was about 15 feet away, and we could see right down into its white gullet. We landed and photographed the fish, and giggled about the dramatic way it came to the fly.

When we got home, Deanna told her mother that we'd had a great time on our trip, that our friend's cabin on the creek was really cool, and that she really liked watching the beaver and the frog ("What beaver? What frog?" I thought). Then, not quite as an afterthought, but in obvious deference to her father, she added "and the fishing was pretty good too."

I have a theory about obsession: that its existence can be confirmed by the frequency with which you think about something when you're not doing it. By this definition, I'm obsessed with hunting and fishing. Deanna is not. She likes them, she is skilled at them, but her life doesn't revolve around them. If she is obsessed, it is with other things, some which might come from her parents – her love of music and words, for instance – and others, like her passion for dance, which seem to have appeared from the air. I have learned not to be disappointed with this. I have accepted the possibility that these things could be as fascinating and rewarding and worthwhile to her as fishing and hunting are to me.

Through most of her youth Deanna was pretty content to hang out with her parents. But last summer when we were planning a family trip to Montana, she began to feel life's pull toward other things. There was discussion about whether she would come with us or stay home and spend time with her friends. In the end, she came, and the trip was a success, but Lynda and I got the distinct sense that the next decision about her participation in such a trip would not be not be ours to make.

We have reached the point where my ability to stir a passion within my daughter for hunting and fishing (and likely for anything else) has ceased. Her future interest in and pursuit of these things are beyond my control. A friend wise in these matters once told me that all we can do is introduce our kids to fishing and shooting when they're young, and then let them live their lives. We shouldn't be surprised if they leave these sports behind while they're focused on schooling, careers, and spouses. But if they were introduced to field sports early, they are likely to come back to them someday, and when they do they might bring our grandchildren with them.

This fall we arranged for Deanna to skip an afternoon of school so we could go bird hunting. She missed a great chance at a cock pheasant, and on the way back to the truck we startled a huge mule deer buck at close range. On the drive home, after I'd teased her about missing the pheasant, she said, "There's always interesting stuff going on out here, isn't there?"

I think she'll be all right.